LEBANON

Sean Sheehan

MARSHALL CAVENDISH
New York • London • Sydney

Reference Edition published 1997 by
Marshall Cavendish Corporation
99 White Plains Road
Tarrytown
New York 10591

© Times Editions Pte Ltd 1997

Originated and designed by
Times Books International, an imprint of
Times Editions Pte Ltd

Printed in Singapore

Library of Congress Cataloging-in-Publication Data:
Sheehan, Sean, 1951–
      Lebanon / Sean Sheehan.
          p.   cm. — (Cultures of the world)
      Includes bibliographical references (p.   ) and index.
      ISBN 0-7614-0283-7 (lib. binding)
      1. Lebanon—Juvenile literature.   I. Title.   II. Series.
   DS80.S53   1997
   956.92—dc20   96–22480
                                              CIP
                                                AC

INTRODUCTION

LEBANON, ONCE PART OF GREATER SYRIA before its partition into Syria, Lebanon, and Palestine, has suffered more than its fair share of the troubles that have afflicted the Middle East. Before 1975, when a terrible civil war erupted, Lebanon was renowned for its sophistication and culture. The history of this small but influential state goes back to the imaginative Phoenicians who created the world's first commercial empire. Lebanon is now once again able to build on its illustrious past.

For too many years Lebanon has been featured as a country at war with itself, beset with kidnappings and terrorist outrages. The 1990s are a time of reconciliation and rebuilding for the Lebanese and an appropriate time for a book that sets out to celebrate Lebanese culture. This book in the *Cultures of the World* series studies the past and present of the country as well as its unique mix of Arabic and Christian cultures.

CONTENTS

The curiously shaped Pigeon Rocks, off the coast of Beirut.

CONTENTS

Lebanon has a long Mediterranean coastline, and most of its citizens live in cities on the coast. These anglers are at the Corniche, a long seaside promenade in Beirut.

GEOGRAPHY

LEBANON IS A COUNTRY at the eastern end of the Mediterranean Sea. Its total land area is 3,950 square miles (10,230 square km), a little smaller than Connecticut. It is bordered on the north and east by Syria, by Israel in the south, and the Mediterranean Sea on the west. The total length of Lebanon's land border is 282 miles (454 km), of which 233 miles (375 km) are shared with Israel and 49 miles (79 km) with Syria. Lebanon's coastline stretches for 140 miles (225 km).

Lebanon is a strip of land 135 miles (217 km) long and only 25–50 miles (40–80 km) wide.

REGIONS

Geographically, Lebanon is a small land with notable contrasts. Before civil war curtailed tourism, tourist information promised that visitors could swim in the Mediterranean in the morning then drive to the mountains to ski in the afternoon.

There are four regions with distinctive features of their own.

COASTAL PLAIN The coastal plain, from Tripoli in the north down to Beirut, midway along the country's coastline, is fairly steep and usually rocky. South of

Beirut there are sandy stretches. The narrow coastal plain is characterized by warm summers, which provide ideal conditions for growing fruit. Groves of orange and olive trees are a common sight and bananas and grapes are also cultivated.

Above and opposite: **Mountains in Lebanon are within easy reach. Buildings hug the slopes and sheep use bridges carved by nature.**

7

Land close to the Anti-Lebanon range cultivated by Armenian refugees.

The Arabic name for Lebanon is Djebel Libnan *("White-as-Milk Mountain") because the peaks of the highest mountains in the country are covered with snow most of the year.*

LEBANON MOUNTAINS Inland, the ground level rises quickly and meets the Lebanon Mountains, one of the country's two high mountain ranges. The Lebanon range follows the coastline from the northern border with Syria as far south as the mouth of the Litani River just north of Tyre. Wherever possible, terraces have been cut into the stone of the mountain and filled with earth to grow vegetables.

BEKAA VALLEY The Bekaa Valley in the northern half of the country is the most fertile of Lebanon's regions, with the richest farm land in the country. Tobacco, mulberries, and cotton are cultivated and aqueducts carry water from the Litani River to the crops.

ANTI-LEBANON RANGE The fourth geographical region is formed by the interior mountains known as the Anti-Lebanon range. These mountains run parallel to the Lebanon Mountains and straddle the eastern border with Syria. In the winter the mountains are characteristically frosty and snowcapped. Apart from shrubs and scattered bush that grow when the weather is warm, there is little natural vegetation.

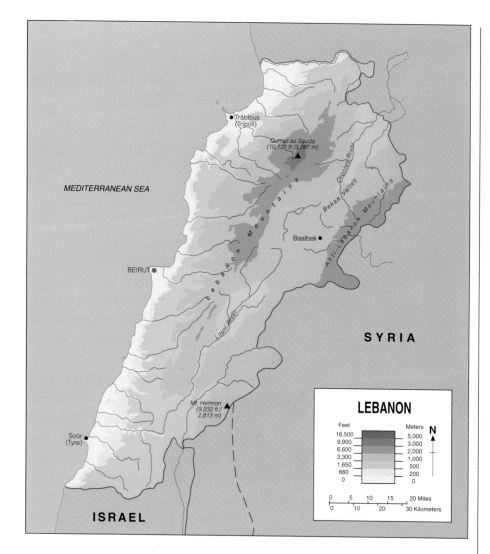

Many springs on
the western slopes
of the Lebanon
Mountains form
small rivers. Other
rivers are seasonal,
being formed in
the wet winters
and drying up in
the dry summers.

RIVERS

The Litani River, which is 90 miles (145 km) long, is the country's longest and most important river. It starts just south of the city of Baalbek and flows south between the two mountain ranges, turning west to meet the sea just north of Tyre. This river is the only one in the Near East that does not cross an international boundary.

The Orontes, Lebanon's other major river, flows north into Syria. Like the Litani, it irrigates agricultural land in the Bekaa Valley.

MOUNT HERMON

The Arabic name for this mountain in the Anti-Lebanon range straddling the border with Syria is "Mountain of the Chief." It has three summits and the highest is 9,232 feet (2,813 meters) above sea level.

For thousands of years the natural grandeur of Mount Hermon has inspired poets and religious mystics. The remains of a number of ancient temples have been found on its slopes, and it is believed to have been the site of the transfiguration of Jesus Christ.

CLIMATE

Lebanon's temperate climate—with some 300 sunny days a year—is a typically Mediterranean one, similar to that of southern California. The chief factor affecting the climate is altitude. Summers are hot and dry and winters warm and moist. Humidity is high along the coast, and Lebanese living there who can afford it move for part of the summer to a second home in the mountains, where the air is drier and cooler.

The Orontes, which irrigates the Bekaa Valley, is called Nahr al-Asi, or the Rebel River, because it flows north through Syria and Turkey before draining into the Mediterranean.

The mountains also serve as an important physical barrier. Rain-bearing clouds blowing in from the Mediterranean west of Lebanon release moisture when they reach the mountains. In the cool months from October through April, when rains fall in torrents along the coast, the mountains are capped in heavy snowfall. This ensures a supply of water when the snow melts later in the year.

The temperature in the summer months rarely exceeds 90°F (32°C) at sea level, while inland in the mountains the temperature is around 68°F (20°C) in the summer. In the winter the temperature on the coast averages 56°F (13°C). The Bekaa Valley is much drier and cooler than the rest of the country; irrigation is necessary to ensure an adequate supply of water to the fields. While Beirut receives an average of 36 inches (91 cm) of rain each year, only 15 inches (38 cm) of rain falls in the Bekaa Valley.

FLORA

Common plants and trees include the poppy, anemones, oak, fir, and cypress. Along the coastal regions there are shrubs known as tamarisks, which can grow in soils with high levels of salt. The scaly leaves of the tamarisk grow on small twigs, giving the tree a feathery appearance, and the stems of one particular species (*Tamarisk mannifera*) produce an edible honey-like substance as a response to attacks by scale insects.

CEDARS OF LEBANON The cedar, native to the eastern Mediterranean and other parts of the world, is an evergreen conifer with a very large trunk and a wide-spreading crown.

The Phoenicians exported the tree to Egypt where, among other things, it was used for boats and coffins, since the wood is believed to repel insects. In Biblical times Lebanon was renowned for its cedar forests, and King Solomon built his palace from the wood of Lebanese cedars. The tree was also considered medicinal as its pitch was used to ease toothache.

Over the centuries cedars have been gradually cut down and destroyed. They once covered vast areas of the country but are now reduced to an area of about 4,200 acres (1,700 hectares), less than 5% of the country's land area.

The most famous stand of cedars still surviving in Lebanon is at Bsharri in the Lebanon Mountains. Here are found the oldest and largest specimens of the tree, reported to be over 2,000 years old. They are, unfortunately, in a very poor state and show little evidence of reproduction. Visitors make huge cuts on the bark and damage the trees, which already suffer from overcrowding, as well as receiving insufficient light and water.

There are plans to try and save the cedars of Lebanon by reforesting them in new and larger areas of the country. Although few traces of the cedar forests remain, the tree is still the country's national emblem and is featured on the national flag.

OLIVES Olives are narrow-leaved, evergreen trees that belong to a botanical family of over 30 different species. The common olive, *Olea europaea*, is native to the Mediterranean area and is grown in Lebanon wherever the climate allows. It is particularly common along the coast

Olives were known to be cultivated in Lebanon as early as the third century B.C. The black fruit of the olive tree contains up to 60% oil, which is extracted by crushing and pressing the fruit. Olive oil, which is used as a cooking and a salad oil, is found in nearly every Lebanese kitchen. The country's high quality olive oil is also an export item.

because the tree is suited to dry summers and cool winters. Ripe and unripe olives have a very bitter taste, but this is removed by soaking olives in an alkaline solution.

FAUNA

The most interesting animal found in Lebanon is the hyrax, a small mammal about the size of a cat that looks like a guinea-pig. It is classified by zoologists as a primitive ungulate (a hoofed mammal), distantly related to elephants. Its resemblance to the elephant can only be seen in its skeleton, its tusk-like incisors, and certain features of its reproductive system.

A number of animals found in Lebanon are threatened with extinction worldwide. They include the grey wolf, the mountain gazelle, a species of pelican, the imperial eagle, and the Mediterranean monk seal.

Migratory birds such as cormorants, flamingos, herons, ducks, and pelicans stop along the marshes of the Bekaa Valley on their way south in the fall and north in the spring. Birds native to Lebanon include song birds like the thrush and nightingale.

CITIES

Lebanon's major cities lie along the coast, and many of them are either ports today or served as ports of call in historical times.

Containers are lined up in neat rows at the dock adjacent to Beirut's sheltered harbor.

BEIRUT Lebanon is one of the most urbanized countries in the Arab world, with well over half of the population living in urban locations of more than 50,000 people. Beirut alone is home to around 40% of the country's population. The city is located on the coastline, at the foot of the Lebanon Mountains.

The capital city of Beirut has remained an important commercial center since over a thousand years before Christ, despite its temporary disappearance for over a century after it was destroyed by a fire in 140 B.C. It has been rebuilt many times since, first by the Romans under Pompey and most recently in the 1990s after a 17-year civil war. It was first conquered by Arabs in A.D. 635, and became an important center of commerce under the Ottomans. The story of the city's development mirrors Lebanon's history.

Beirut is a major seaport and handles the bulk of the country's imports and exports. The city has important rail, road, and air connections to other parts of the country as well as to other cities in the Middle East.

TRIPOLI Tripoli (or Trâblous), the second most important city in Lebanon, is situated in the northwest of the country. Like Beirut, it is an important seaport and its port district is situated on a small peninsula some two miles (3 km) from the inland city center. Tripoli is also the terminal for a major oil pipeline from Iraq, and oil refining is a major industry there.

The city of Tripoli has an ancient heritage. It was founded in 700 B.C. by the Phoenicians. In A.D. 638 it was taken by Muslims and held until 1109, when Crusaders conquered and occupied the city. It has a famous old Frankish castle, St Giles. In 1289 the city was destroyed by the Egyptians, but it was later rebuilt and became an important city under the Ottomans.

Today its major industries are soap manufacturing, tobacco cultivation, and sponge fishing.

The name Tripoli has its roots in two Greek words: "tri" (three) and "poli" (cities). Today, it consists of two parts: El Mina is the outlying port and the main city is two miles inland.

SPONGE FISHING

The sponges that occupy a place near most kitchen sinks and on every supermarket shelf are the skeletons of a marine species found throughout the world. And if your kitchen has one of the best quality sponges it is possible the skeleton belonged to a marine animal scooped out of the Mediterranean by a Lebanese fisherman.

Sponges are multicellular animals whose surface layer of cells covers an inner layer of flagellated cells (flagella are whip-like appendages) that move water through the animal, collecting food and providing a form of propulsion. There are numerous varieties of sponges throughout the world, but those found in the Mediterranean Sea are rated the best because of the softness of their skeletons.

Sponges are collected by fishermen who dive into the water for them. The animal tissue is left to decompose before the skeletal tissue, which does not decompose, is washed and bleached. It is then cut into the familiar blocks that eventually find their way onto the shelves of your local supermarket.

Zahle, on the slopes of the Lebanon Mountains, is a market town and resort famous for its flowers and vineyards.

SIDON Another city with a castle that dates back to the Crusades is Sidon (also known as Sayda), although the 13th century ruins are by no means the earliest reminder of Sidon's ancient heritage. Christ preached a sermon in Sidon on one of his journeys, and a number of important archeological finds have been unearthed in the area. Phoenician burial sites, cut out of the bare rock, have been found close to the city.

Sidon is situated in the southwest of the country. It is commercially important as a center for the export of olive oil and fruit. Tobacco and figs are cultivated in the surrounding countryside.

TYRE Another ancient city is Tyre (also known as Soûr), and it is probably far older than Sidon. Tyre is said to have provided the 80,000 craftsmen who built King Solomon's palace in the 10th century B.C. The famous ancient Greek historian, Herodotus, refers to an oral tradition that traced the city's origins back to the 28th century B.C. This is in keeping with Greek mythology, which records how a daughter of a king of Tyre captured the heart of Zeus. After falling in love he escaped with her to a continent in the west that he named after her. Her name was Europa.

Tyre was the most important city in ancient Phoenicia. The Phoenicians extracted a highly valued dye from shellfish, which became known as

Tyrian purple. Cloth of this color was exclusive at the time. Tyre was captured by Muslims in the 7th century. In the 12th century, it was captured by Crusaders, who held it until 1291, when Muslim rule was reestablished. During 1982, as a result of a war between the Arabs and Israel, Tyre was badly damaged. Today, it is still being rebuilt in places.

BYBLOS Byblos, or Jubayl, now a very small town some 20 miles (32 km) north of Beirut, is a serious contender for the claim to be the oldest town in the world. There are records of trade with Byblos in 2800 B.C., when the Egyptians arrived to barter for the papyrus they used for making a form of paper. It is said that the Greek word for book (*biblos*)—hence the word "bible"—comes from the name of this town. Near Byblos are unique "wall tombs," shafts quarried into the rock as burial sites, and ancient Egyptian alabaster vases found in them give some idea of how old they are.

Byblos is home to the first Crusader castle built in the Levant, a name given to the countries on the eastern shores of the Mediterranean Sea.

Byblos, a famous harbor in historical times, is today a quiet fishing town.

OTHER CITIES Some cities have grown in importance only recently, while others will always be important as historical sites. Junia, once a village, is now a city with a thriving port just north of Beirut. The ancient city of Baalbek in the foothills of the Anti-Lebanon Mountains is famous for its Roman ruins, including temples once dedicated to the Roman gods Jupiter and Bacchus. Zahle, which lies on the slopes of the Lebanon Mountains, is a resort whose popularity is evident by the numerous cafés doing a brisk business by the side of its stream.

HISTORY

IN THE PAST FEW YEARS Lebanon has been literally rebuilding itself, an ironic and tragic fact for a country that is steeped in thousands of years of history. Indeed, Lebanon's history accompanies some of the earliest and most important steps in the development of civilization.

EARLY TRADERS

The little that is known about the early inhabitants of the land now called Lebanon applies to the Levant, or lands bordering the eastern shores of the Mediterranean. This region has rich alluvial soil, which would have attracted the Middle East's first farmers.

Rich land is also found in the Bekaa Valley, and here too early farmers settled down after migrating from Mesopotamia, home to the very early

Opposite: **Sphinx-like carving among the ruins in Byblos, a city that traded with Egypt between the 20th and 18th centuries** B.C.

Left: **The temple of Jupiter stands among the ruins of the temple complex the Romans built at Heliopolis (now called Baalbek) around the second century** A.D.

A king of Tyre and Sidon, Luli, fled from the Assyrians in the fleet of the Phoenician navy. The Phoenicians were early colonizers and traders, and their skill in navigation was well-known.

Sumerian and Babylonian civilizations. The excavation of a clay, kiln-fired sculpture dating back to 3000 B.C. is evidence of this. It is a figure of Astarte, also known as Ishtar, who was originally a Mesopotamian mother-goddess of love and war. Other terra cotta figures from around this period have also been found; nearly all are of nude female figures.

Finds of terra cotta figures bearing elaborate hairstyles and jewelry show the influence of ancient Egyptian culture on the Levant. Pharaoh Ramses II (1304–1237 B.C.) passed through Lebanon in his war against the Hittites, whom he defeated in modern-day Syria. The Obelisk Temple at Byblos clearly shows an Egyptian influence in its style and design.

In the ancient town of Byblos excavations have revealed town walls that date back to the Amorite period. "Amorite" is a general term for early groups of Semitic people who established communities in the Levant in Old Testament times. Amorite settlements along the coast were naturally engaged in local maritime trade and would also have traded with inland communities in what is now Syria and Jordan. Out of such a background there developed the first known commercial empire on earth.

PHOENICIA

The word "Phoenicia" is said to be derived from a Greek word for purple, referring to the purple dye that once made Tyre famous. The city of Tyre was the Phoenician capital, home to a commercial empire that stretched

A THEORY ABOUT A DWARF-GOD WITH A BEARD

It is possible that the Phoenicians discovered America some 2,000 years before either the Vikings in the 10th century or the expedition 500 hundred years later led by Christopher Columbus. The evidence for putting forward this theory is partly based on the known seafaring prowess of the Phoenicians. They are believed to have sailed down the coast of Africa and probably reached the southwest of Britain. Research has also revealed similarities between pre-Columbian America and Mediterranean civilization. There are parallels in metallurgy, agriculture, mathematics, and language between Phoenician culture and those of the Olmecs and Mayas of the Americas.

An example that is given to support this claim of a cultural link is a dwarflike god, Bes, whose image adorned the prows of Phoenician ships. A "twin" American dwarflike god has also been found in statues of Olmec culture in Central America and the Mayas of South America. What gives some weight to this example is that the American god is always shown with a beard and in pre-Columbian American culture men did not grow beards. The bearded dwarf, it is claimed, crossed the Atlantic with his Phoenician admirers.

By 1000 B.C. the Phoenicians had invented the alphabet.
The ancient Greek historian Herodotus wrote that the Phoenicians were the first people to sail around Africa, which they may have done around 600 B.C.

westward to the Straits of Gibraltar and included the founding of Carthage, an ancient city-state, in the 9th century B.C. The Phoenicians traded linen, metal, glass, wood, ivory, and precious stones. Sometime around the 8th century B.C. the Phoenician cities came into conflict with Assyria, another ancient kingdom, and were weakened as a result. Subsequently they came under the influence of other powerful groups like the Babylonians, the Persians, and later the Romans. As part of the Roman empire, Lebanon was Christianized.

THE ROMANS

In 64 B.C. the Roman general Pompey the Great conquered Phoenicia after clearing the Mediterranean Sea of pirates. Using what is now Lebanon as a base he went on to wage a successful war against the kings of Armenia and Syria. The whole region, including Jerusalem, became part of the Roman empire.

The Crusaders built impressive castles east of the Mediterranean, such as this one in Sidon.

The Romans wanted quality timber for their ships and buildings and they found just what they needed in the forests of modern-day Lebanon. They kept guard over the forests and built roads to transport logs to the coast from where they could be shipped back to Rome. The Romans are famous for the roads they built and carefully maintained by carrying out repairs whenever necessary. Roman milestones, recording the completion of road repairs, have been found in Lebanon.

THE CRUSADERS

Before the Crusaders arrived, the mountainous region of Lebanon known as Mount Lebanon was a refuge for persecuted minorities. The Christian Maronites settled there from the 7th century and the Muslim Druze occupied the southern part of the mountains from the 11th century.

The Crusaders, who came mostly from France, Germany, and Italy, were called Franks by the Arabs. The first Crusade expedition arrived in 1099 and the last one remained until the 14th century. The aim of the Crusades was to secure Christian rule over the Muslim-controlled holy places of the eastern Mediterranean. Christian communities had been finding it increasingly difficult to withstand the growing Islamization of the country. The Crusaders helped ensure their survival.

HISTORY IN STONE

Lebanon's long history is written in stone monuments and the remains can be seen today. Outside Beirut is a Roman aqueduct and Roman ruins are extensive at Baalbek. Phoenician artifacts have been excavated in Beirut, Byblos, and Tyre. Crusaders' castles are still standing near Byblos.

More legendary than historic is a structure at Nebi Yunis claimed to be the tomb of Noah. There is also a small chapel-mosque at al-Khadr where St. George is said to have slain the dragon.

MUSLIM RULE

The caliphs were religious and secular successors to Mohammed, the founder of Islam, and under the second caliph the first expansion of Islam outside of Arabia took place. In A.D. 630 the Arabs conquered Syria and annexed most of modern-day Lebanon, turning it into a military and political region governed from Damascus. A Damascus-based dynasty, the Umayyads ("oo-MY-ahdz"), ruled until 750 before it was forcibly replaced by a rival caliphate. The new caliphs, the Abbasids ("ah-BAH-sidz"), established themselves in Baghdad.

The Christians were allowed to retain their religion, but they were discriminated against and lost social and political power. In 759 and again in 760 there were revolts by Christian communities, but the rebellions were easily repressed.

As a result of the violent struggle between the Umayyads and the Abbasids, local dynasties emerged in Lebanon. A more centralised Muslim rule, however, was established again after the rise of the Mamluks, also known as Mamelukes, who overthrew the Abbasids in 1250.

Saladin, a famous 12th century Muslim leader, fought against the Crusaders. By 1300, other than their fortress-like castles, little remained of the Crusaders' presence in the eastern Mediterranean.

Deir el Kamar, an old Christian town in the mountains southeast of Beirut, was the Ottoman capital. Some buildings in this town were designed by Tuscan architects imported in the 17th century.

THE OTTOMANS

The Mamluk Muslim dynasties were still ruling Lebanon when, early in the 16th century, the Ottoman Turks arrived on the scene. The Ottomans conquered Lebanon and other regions of the eastern Mediterranean coast. Ottoman rule was based on economics, not religion, and they allowed non-Muslim communities to practice their own religions as long as they paid their taxes.

The more powerful local families were put in charge of collecting the taxes and they became the basis for influential dynasties that began to emerge in the late 16th and 17th centuries. Descendants of some of these powerful families still dominate Lebanese politics. Two main dynasties controlled the political scene: the Maans and, later, the Shihabs. They formed various alliances with different Muslim and Christian groups, chiefly the Druzes and Maronites respectively, but switching allegiances between the different power groups led to an instability in Lebanese politics that boded ill for the future.

Constant rivalry between Muslim and Christian groups took the form of religious conflicts, but they often disguised deeper economic inequalities between different groups of people. Increasing animosity between landlords and peasants and political differences between Druze and Maronite groups came to a head in 1858 and a fierce civil war raged for two years. It ended with an apparent victory for the Druze, but in 1859 foreign troops from European powers and the Ottoman empire arrived in the country and established a new administration. This ensured that a Christian ruler governed the country, while Lebanon remained part of the Ottoman empire. This state lasted until World War I (1914–1918).

In April 1920, Lebanon and Syria were placed under the French Mandate and General Henri Gouraud (below).

FRENCH RULE

During World War I, the Ottoman empire supported Germany. After the war, the victors (Britain, France, and Russia) divided up the territories that had formerly belonged to the vanquished, and the French emerged as the new rulers of Lebanon.

The French created the modern borders of Lebanon and established its identity as a separate country. Before this the territory had always been part of larger provinces governed by empires based in Rome, Damascus, Medina, and Constantinople. The French brought together the Muslim coastal areas and the inland Christian mountain area into one administrative region.

Many Muslims were reluctant to accept their new identity as Lebanese because they saw the new country as being Western and Christian. The French and the Maronites supported one another, and when the country became independent in 1926, the Christians were left in a politically powerful position. The French created one country, but not a unified people. The basic conflict between Christian groups who looked to the West and Muslim groups who looked to the Arab world was an underlying cause of a civil war that would return Lebanon to the fractured state that existed before the French took over.

The presence of various ethnic groups demanding greater political representation led to civil unrest after independence. A pro-Arab rebel group, whose members are seen above, was led by Kamal Jumblatt, a Lebanese politician.

INDEPENDENCE

In 1926 the Lebanese republic was formed and a constitution was drawn up. The French were happy to accept this until 1943, when the Lebanese parliament declared independence. France imprisoned the president and prime minister. To protest this action, there was a general strike and an uprising. Under pressure from Britain and the United States, France backed down.

As often happened in history, the colonial power in Lebanon left behind a state of instability and conflict that it had largely created in the first place. A power-sharing system was set up in which government posts were divided between representatives of the main religious groups. A compromise was reached: the Christians renounced allegiance to the West, while the Muslims renounced union with Syria or other Arab states. The effect, however, was to institutionalize the differences between the religious groups, and because the Christians were given a disproportionate amount of power, there was bitter resentment on the part of the increasing number of poor Shiite Muslims.

The powerful Christian lobby began to express a wish to ally itself with the West and distance itself from the neighboring Arab world. Muslims naturally wished for closer cooperation with other Arab states, and there were two coups, in 1949 and 1961, aimed at forming a union with Syria. In 1958 the first outbreak of war in Lebanon occurred when Lebanese people responded to the pan-Arab call of Egyptian President Nasser. The United States intervened for the first time, and in Lebanon President Camille Chamoun was replaced by General Faud Chebab.

Former president Camille Chamoun (second from the right) and newly elected president General Faud Chehab with some government representatives after the election in Beirut in August 1958.

In 1970, the Palestine Liberation Organization (PLO) moved its headquarters to Lebanon after being expelled from Jordan. As the Arab-Israeli conflict deepened, Palestinians expelled from Israel sought refuge in Lebanon, where other Palestinians had fled when the state of Israel was first created. Raids were organized across the border into the Jewish state, adding to the tensions that were beginning to tear the country apart.

ISRAEL INVADES

In 1978 Israel invaded the southern part of the country in support of the Christians. It invaded again in 1982. The assassination of the Christian president-elect, Bashir Gemayel, in 1982 brought an Israeli advance to Beirut and the city was kept under siege for three months. The PLO were seriously threatened by the Israelis and were forced to withdraw from Beirut under protection from an international army.

When West Beirut was occupied by the Israeli army, a massacre of Palestinians by Christian militia took place in the Sabra and Shatila refugee camps. This led to the deployment of United Nations peacekeeping forces. The Israeli invasion left 12,000 Lebanese and Palestinians dead, 40,000 wounded, 300,000 homeless, and 100,000 without shelter.

An armed militia man stands watch over Beirut's Canon Square. During the civil war a 40 mile (64 km) stretch of coast road had 16 checkpoints, each governed by a different militia that was at war with the other 15.

CIVIL WAR

In 1975 fighting erupted between Muslim and Christian factions. It began when shots were fired into a congregation where the Christian president was worshiping. The car used in the attack was identified as belonging to a Palestinian group. A few hours later a bus carrying Palestinians was fired on by Christian soldiers and 27 were left dead. A civil war had begun.

In the following year the Palestine Liberation Organization joined forces with the Muslims.

In 1983, more than 300 American and French troops were killed by terrorist bombs and Western forces eventually pulled out of the country. This allowed the civil conflict to erupt once more. Westerners in Beirut became the target of Muslim kidnappers in 1984, and in 1987 Syrian troops occupied Beirut. In the south of the country the Israeli army continued to do battle with Palestinian troops. Beirut became a divided city: East Beirut was Christian, West Beirut was Muslim. The border line between the two became known as the Green Line and it was often the scene of fierce fighting. The country was governed by a bewildering array of militias, each of which controlled their own territory.

Over the next two years the country teetered on the brink of collapse. The rival Muslim and Christian groups could not agree on who should be president.

PEACE AT LAST—ALMOST

Towards the end of 1989 negotiations between the rival power groups led to a new constitution that gave increased power to Muslims. With Syrian support, the Taif Agreement, named after a place in Saudi Arabia where the leaders met, was brought into effect. In 1991 nearly all the Western hostages were released. The Green Line dividing Beirut was dismantled and young people were able to visit the other side of their capital for the first time.

In 1992 voting for a new National Assembly took place for the first time in 20 years—17 years after the first incidents that led to the civil war. The elections were, however, boycotted by some Christian parties.

Southern Lebanon remains in a state of war. Israeli troops still occupy territory and radical Muslims continue to use southern Lebanon as a base for attacking Israel. Civilians continue to suffer and innocent Lebanese periodically fall victim to Israeli shelling. Syrian troops are still in Lebanon and many Lebanese remain concerned about the power wielded by the Syrians.

Amin Gemayel (below), president of Lebanon from 1982 until 1988, when the civil war was at its height. General Michel Aoun, who succeeded him, objected to Syrian involvement in government, and was evicted in 1990.

GOVERNMENT

IN OCTOBER 1990, CIVIL WAR ENDED and Lebanon began to rebuild its political institutions. The most important difference is that now Muslims have a greater say in the running of their country. After the end of the French mandate in 1943, political control of the country was always in the hands of a Christian presidency. Now, political authority is in the hands of a Muslim prime minister and there is a more equitable Christian-Muslim representation in the 128-deputy parliament.

THE CONSTITUTION

Although Lebanon became independent in 1943, the constitution (which has been amended several times) dates from 1926. Lebanon is a republic, with universal suffrage, which means that every adult has the right to vote.

The formal head of government is the prime minister, who is chosen by the president in consultation with the members of the National Assembly. By custom the president is a Maronite Christian, the prime minister is a Sunni Muslim,

Above: **A policeman patrols the streets of post-civil war Beirut.**

Opposite: **Members of the South Lebanese Army (SLA) in an armored personnel carrier patrol the countryside in search of insurgents.**

and the speaker of the National Assembly is a Shiite Muslim. This tripartite division based on religion dates back to 1943 when the country first achieved independence. At that time an agreement was made that all government bodies would be proportioned on the basis of six Christians to five Muslims. This division was always unfair because Christians did not make up a majority of the population. It gave undue power to the Christians and caused conflict. This eventually led to the civil war that ended with a new constitution giving Muslims their proper majority say in the running of the country.

Foreign armies continue to occupy Lebanon: the Israeli-controlled South Lebanese Army patrols the hot terrain of the south on foot, while Syrian forces are deployed in Beirut, north Lebanon, and the Bekaa Valley.

UNSOLVED PROBLEMS

A number of unsolved problems make the task of governing Lebanon particularly difficult. They are not the sort of problems most governments have to deal with. The basic problem is that different groups within the country still maintain their own armies and the central government has no authority over them.

The Lebanese Armed Forces represents the new government order that emerged after the civil war. In the early 1990s it was very busy confiscating a vast array of weapons used by the various militias during the civil war. Despite this, the radical Shiite party, Hizbollah, still retains most of its weapons, and elements of the Hizbollah party remain outside the mainstream of conventional political life.

Israel continues to occupy an area in southern Lebanon through its control of a militia known as the South Lebanese Army (SLA). The SLA is in effect an arm of the Israeli army and as such it occupies and controls

MR. MIRACLE

Rafiq al-Hariri, who became Lebanon's prime minister after the end of the civil war, was nicknamed Mr. Miracle by Lebanese newspapers. He is an extremely rich man, one of the world's 100 wealthiest people, and has set himself the task of spearheading the rebuilding of his country. He has put $100 million into an investment project for the rebuilding of Beirut, and since 1982 he has paid university fees for 15,000 Lebanese studying at home and abroad.

It has been said that he will indeed have to be a Mr. Miracle to survive as Lebanon's leading politician. Many political leaders have been assassinated by rival groups and Rafiq al-Hariri requires massive security to thwart the attempts on his life. He personally employs 40 private bodyguards and drives in a convoy of six armored Mercedes accompanied by armed soldiers in other vehicles. The central government offices are installed with blast-resistant armor plating and bulletproof glass.

In mid-1995 Rafiq al-Hariri began his second three-year term as Lebanon's prime minister.

In 1991, Christian, Druze, and Shiite militias gave their weapons to the government army. The Palestinians refused, saying that their weapons were used against Israelis and not the Lebanese.

the southern border with Israel and about 12 miles (20 km) of Lebanese territory. Israeli troops, numbering about 1,000, have been in southern Lebanon since June 1982.

Syria also maintains a force of over 30,000 troops in Beirut, north Lebanon, and the Bekaa Valley. Syrian troops have been in Lebanon since October 1976. Under the terms of the 1989 agreement that ended the civil war, Syrian troops were supposed to be redeployed from the coastal centers of population to the Bekaa Valley, but this has not yet taken place. The presence of Syrian troops in Lebanon, and the unwillingness of the government to press the issue, is resented by many Lebanese.

Palestinian groups also maintain their own authority in the refugee camps that are found throughout the country.

Hizbollah posters plaster the walls in Beirut.

THE LAST VIOLENT FRONTIER

The 9 mile (15 km) wide enclave of South Lebanon is a remnant of the Arab-Israeli conflict that has scarred the Middle East for the last 30 years. About 1,000 Israeli soldiers and 3,000 South Lebanese Army troops hold onto this portion of Lebanon to prevent attacks on the Jewish state by pro-Iranian Hizbollah guerrillas. Drivers of vehicles crossing the checkpoint between Lebanon and South Lebanon are suspect unless they have at least one passenger, preferably a woman or a child. Otherwise they are seen as potential Hizbollah suicide bombers.

The 150,000 inhabitants of South Lebanon will be denied the benefits of other Lebanese until the Israelis can bring themselves to withdraw. The SLA soldiers, despised by other Arabs as collaborators with Israel, are living a precarious existence and undoubtedly many of them will have to leave the country permanently once Israeli support is withdrawn.

Only when South Lebanon is finally reunited with Lebanon will the Middle East peace process be completed.

HIZBOLLAH

Hizbollah is a radical Shiite Muslim organization. It has its roots with the poorest minority of Arabs living in Lebanon. The poor Arabs of Lebanon were politicized by the impact of Israel's invasions in 1978 and 1982 and Hizbollah was the name given to their political organization. The growth of Hizbollah has been funded by large amounts of money from Iran.

Today, Hizbollah is engaged in both peaceful politics and armed conflict with Israel in South Lebanon. It has representatives in the new political system and its funding from Iran allows it to develop and maintain an extensive social welfare program for the poorest sections of Lebanese society. Much-needed hospitals, schools, and food shops are run by Hizbollah and give assistance that the central government is not yet able to provide.

It is thought likely that at some time in the future Israel will withdraw from its self-declared security zone in South Lebanon. This is likely to be part of a broader peace settlement with Syria. When—or if—this happens Hizbollah would have little choice but to hand in its weapons. It would then become a proper political party. The only alternative would be to maintain violent opposition to Israel without the support of the Syrian or the Lebanese government.

Men carry the bodies of Muslims at a Hizbollah funeral in Beirut.

HUMAN RIGHTS AND JUSTICE

After so many years of civil war it is not surprising that human rights have suffered. The law does require a suspect to be released after 48 hours unless charges are made, but this is not always followed in practice. Persons on trial do have the right to a lawyer, but only if they can afford to pay for one. This means, of course, that poor people are at a serious disadvantage in the courtroom.

There are a number of different courts. Besides the regular civilian court there is also a military court, which handles all cases involving members of military groups. There are also religious tribunals for the various Muslim and Christian denominations. These handle disputes involving marriage and inheritance.

In the refugee camps, Palestinian groups operate their courts. So too does Hizbollah, the Islamic militia, and in these cases Islamic law is applied. This sometimes conflicts with the laws of Lebanon.

THE PRESIDENT

The current president of Lebanon is Elias Hrawi, a Maronite Christian, and he has been the president since almost a year before the end of the civil war in 1990. At the end of 1995 parliament extended his term for another three years. This has been criticized as undemocratic because under Lebanon's constitution a new president would have been elected, with the incumbent barred from reelection.

Elias Hrawi is regarded as a pro-Syrian politician. Opposition politicians claim he would not have been allowed to stay in office without Syrian support. Hrawi signed a treaty with Syria on May 22, 1991, under the terms of which Syria recognized Lebanon as an independent state. However, issues concerning defense, internal security, and economic and foreign affairs were to be decided by joint commissions of both countries.

ECONOMY

LEBANON IS MAKING A BRAVE ATTEMPT to rise above the economic chaos created by the long years of civil war. In the process of restructuring its economy, it is showing the world that it does have a future as a nation. At regular intervals throughout the 1980s Lebanon was being written off as a nation, and there were predictions that the country would break up into an unstable number of mini-states. This has not happened and Lebanon is busy building a new economy as a nation state.

PRECIVIL WAR ECONOMY

Before 1975 Lebanon ranked as one of the 35 upper middle-income countries of the world. The country's economy was anchored in trade, and two-thirds of the national income came from trade, banking, and tourism. Foreign visitors were attracted to the combination of a pleasant climate and a wealth of historical remains. This kind of economy depends on stability. Not surprisingly, then, the civil war destroyed the economy. Tourists and investors don't want to risk their lives or money in a country at war with itself.

Another problem was caused by the loss of central government control. A number of regions were controlled by local militias. The central government was unable to collect taxes, so the years of factional fighting have seriously damaged Lebanon's economy. The result is rising unemployment and a very high rate of inflation, serious disadvantages for those who are poor to begin with. As a result, the poor get poorer and the rich get richer. The current rate of inflation is around 35%.

Opposite: **Blacksmiths at Shatila Camp straighten twisted reinforcing steel rods reclaimed from bombed buildings.**

Below: **The desolation of Martyrs' Place in Beirut is a reminder of the civil war, but a clear sign that tourism is returning to Lebanon is this boy selling paintings of Martyrs' Place before the war.**

Public notices are plastered on the walls still standing amid the rubble.

HARD TIMES

For many Lebanese, dealing with the peace of the 1990s is as demanding and draining as was surviving the fighting of the 1970s and 1980s. Due to the high rate of inflation, prices are constantly increasing and not in line with the average monthly wage of around $130. Electricity is still only available for fixed periods each day, and many people cannot afford private generators so they have to manage with batteries or candles. More than one in three Lebanese is unemployed.

The divisions between the rich and poor are increasing. The richest fifth of the population receive 55% of the country's private income; the poorest fifth receive only 4%. Educational and health care of a reasonable standard is mainly restricted to those who can afford to pay for it.

Rebuilding Beirut is a massive task that begins with demolishing bombed out buildings and removing the rubble.

HORIZON 2000

Horizon 2000 is the name of the government's masterplan to rebuild Lebanon. The plan was first announced in 1993, about 18 months after the last shell of the civil war destroyed one more building of old Beirut.

By the end of the civil war the country's infrastructure was in a serious state of disrepair. Only one in three of the country's telephones was working and electricity was restricted to six hours a day in Beirut. Outside the capital, electricity was nonexistent in many places. Water was also in short supply and when it was available it was often polluted.

The total cost of Horizon 2000 was initially estimated at $13 billion, and this figure is certain to double or even triple over the coming years. Just over one third of this amount is planned to come from loans and aid from other countries; the rest will come from government revenue. This presents a major problem because the country is presently making about $4 billion a year.

The plan to rebuild the city center of Beirut is a controversial one. The city's central area was previously the zone that bridged the east and west

REBUILDING A COUNTRY

Restoring working order to Lebanon is an uphill task. While fundamental progress is being made in some areas, the task seems insurmountable in others.

- Between mid-1993 and the beginning of 1995 over one million new telephone lines were installed.
- In the same period of time the country's six sewage treatment plants were repaired and reopened.
- Over 1,000 schools need to be substantially rebuilt.
- Out of the 24 hospitals in the country, 17 need substantial rebuilding.
- A new runway and terminal buildings are planned for Beirut International Airport.

LOSSES AND GAINS

On the minus side:

- The Lebanese currency has been grossly devalued. In 1980 one US dollar bought just under 3.5 Lebanese pounds on the open currency market. By 1993 one US dollar could purchase over 1,500 pounds.
- In the first 10 years of the civil war (1975–1985) income per capita fell from $1,900 to $980.

Among the pluses:

- In the first two years of peace (1990–1992) industrial exports increased from $190 million to $420 million.
- In the same period the number of ships docking in Beirut port increased from under 700 to over 3,000.

sides of the divided city during the civil war. So many buildings had been damaged that well over half of the area had to be completely demolished and cleared before rebuilding could begin. The plan is to restore Beirut to its pre-1975 status as a major international business and banking center. Critics say this is an unnecessary ambition given the need to rebuild living conditions for the ordinary citizens of the country.

MAKING A CHOICE

Lebanon faces many challenges as it tries to reconstruct a viable economy that will provide work for its citizens. The major challenge is to find the huge amount of money needed to get various projects off the ground. The government of Lebanon has decided to use private capital for most of the important rebuilding and restructuring programs.

A good example of the government's approach is the program to rebuild Beirut. One aspect of this was dealing with the large number of owners and tenants who had claims on the land and buildings.

An airplane of the national Middle East Airlines taxis to position at the Beirut International Airport. The MEA was the largest nongovernment employer in Lebanon before the civil war.

An estimated 50,000 people had claims and they were all affected by a law the government passed to deal with this situation. Under this law property owners could choose to sell their land to the company set up to manage the entire rebuilding project. The only alternative was to reclaim their land and carry out all necessary reconstruction within a fixed period of time.

Some people say this is unfair because owners without sufficient funds had little choice but to sell their land to the company. The large profits expected to flow from the new Beirut city center will never be shared with the original owners of the buildings and land. Instead, private investors have been invited to buy shares in the project. Many of these investors are foreign companies and they have effectively purchased property that once belonged to Lebanese citizens. Critics of this policy point out that it is typical of a government more interested in creating profits for private companies than in creating an economic climate where all Lebanese will share in the hoped-for prosperity. The gap between the small number of rich people and the mass of poor people is said to be increasing as a result.

43

NATURAL RESOURCES

Lebanon is not rich in mineral resources. Lignite (known as brown coal) is mined and there are supplies of gypsum. There are small amounts of phosphates, copper, and coal.

The country's fast-flowing rivers, especially the Litani, are being developed for hydroelectric power and the irrigation of the surrounding agricultural land.

AGRICULTURE

The typical agricultural use of land in Lebanon involves the cutting of terraces on mountain slopes. This is particularly favored in the Bekaa Valley where over 80% of the total land area is used for agriculture, mainly grain cultivation. The typical farm in the Bekaa Valley is just over 12 acres (less than 5 hectares).

Apart from grains (mostly wheat), fruit is the most common farm output: citrus fruit, figs, grapes, mulberries, apples, and bananas are the most important. Vegetables and olives are also found on most farms.

The long dry summer months cause a shortage of water for farmers who, over the centuries, have fine-tuned all available means of irrigation. The most ambitious attempt to channel water to where it is most needed involves using the country's longest river, the Litani. The project should have been completed two decades ago but the constant state of war in the country has caused substantial delays.

NARCOTICS

Lebanon has been a major player in the production and distribution of narcotics, primarily opium and hashish. Both the poppy and cannabis, from which opium and hashish respectively are produced, are cultivated in the Bekaa Valley. Raw opium and cocaine are also smuggled into Lebanon for processing, before being smuggled out again to the United States and Europe. Lebanon's traditional banking secrecy laws are believed to help illegal organizations involved in money laundering operations arising from drugs.

In recent years the government has attempted to eradicate the illicit drug trade. It is estimated that the country now produces 80% less opium (less than one metric ton) than in the early 1990s. It is also estimated that the cultivation of cannabis has dropped by 50%.

The ultimate success of operations designed to eliminate the trade in narcotics depends on convincing farmers to switch to the cultivation of staple crops. This in turn depends on the provision of funds to compensate farmers for the substitution of crops.

Above and opposite: **All family members help at harvesting time in the Bekaa Valley. One harvester bites off a piece of gourd to prove how tasty it is.**

Above: **A man buys up metal frames to resell.**

Opposite: **Jewelry is a major export product in Lebanon.**

INDUSTRY

The country is gradually reestablishing the industries that gave regular employment before the interruptions caused by civil war. The main industries are food processing, chemicals, and textiles. Most industrial enterprises are small-scale, employing only half a dozen people. They are concentrated around Beirut.

ENTREPRENEURS

The civil war did not dampen the Lebanese spirit of enterprise. Some people who fled Beirut during the war, leaving behind thriving business concerns, simply picked up the pieces when they returned. A few Lebanese who had lost everything they owned started from scratch in a different line of business. Disaster brought opportunities for new entrepreneurs who scoured war-torn areas for twisted steel rods and frames, then sold these to buyers who had a use for them. Recycling was the short-term answer to the shortage of materials in Lebanon.

IMPORTS AND EXPORTS

Due to its lack of natural resources, Lebanon has always had to import far more than it exports. Consumer goods account for a large share of the imports, along with machinery, transport equipment, and petroleum products.

Despite its trade imbalance, prior to the civil war Lebanon was not in danger of falling into increasing debt. It had been able to earn a lot of money from what economists call invisible earnings. Tourists visiting the country spent their foreign currency and this was a major source of invisible earnings. Even more profitable was income earned through financial dealings involving banking and insurance. The country is now trying to rebuild these industries.

The main exports are agricultural products, chemicals, and precious and semiprecious metals and jewelry. The main countries that trade with Lebanon are neighboring Middle East states, France, Germany, and the United States.

BANKING CAPITAL OF THE MIDDLE EAST?

Before civil war began in 1975, Beirut held the undisputed claim of being the banking capital of the Middle East. The country's ambition is to reestablish this claim within the next 10 years. It is not an unrealistic aim, partly because in the interim no other city in the Middle East was able to even approach the status that Beirut once commanded.

Part of Beirut's success as a trusted financial center lay in its banking secrecy laws. Beirut and Zurich were equally renowned when it came to

The solid front of Junia's financial area, about 10 miles (16 km) north of Beirut.

offering investors the highest degree of security and protection. At a time when most of the Middle East, unlike Western Europe, suffered from an "image problem" in terms of internal stability, the financial institutions based in Beirut were able to offer a haven of international security and trust. Beirut's banks attracted billions of investors' dollars from neighboring countries. As a result of this, over one quarter of Lebanon's national income was based on services to non-Lebanese.

There are positive signs that Beirut is going to be able to rebuild its image as the Arab capitalist engine-room. Some of the millions of dollars that flowed out of the country after 1975 are trickling back into secret bank accounts. The famous Casino du Liban, once an icon of Beirut's status as the social and business hub of the Arab world, is being rebuilt. A sure sign that Beirut is recapturing international trust and recognition is the fact that familiar American fast-food chains have opened branches in the city. One fast-food chain, in particular, has plans to open 17 branches by the end of 1996.

Many of the factors that supported Beirut's successful image as the capitalist hub of the Middle East are still there. In particular, the port of Beirut, once the most important in the eastern Mediterranean, is regaining its dominant role as the conduit for trade involving countries like Syria, Iraq, and Iran.

Beirut remains the financial center of Lebanon, while other coastal cities play a greater role than ever before as shipping centers. The port of Sidon, or Sayda (above), is also an important terminal for oil refining.

LEBANESE

LEBANESE CITIZENS TODAY are mostly descendants of a mixture of people—the Phoenicians, Greeks, Crusaders, and Arabs—who at different times occupied the country. It was only after World War I (1914–1918), when Lebanon began to define itself as a separate state under French rule, that people even began to think of themselves as Lebanese. In the previous centuries, under Ottoman rule, people thought of themselves as belonging first to the Ottoman state, then to the region in which they lived.

It was also under French rule that the idea of belonging to a religious group was politicized. And since 1975, when the civil war began, a person was defined as a Muslim Lebanese or a Christian Lebanese. The notion of one country called Lebanon and one set of citizens almost disappeared.

Only in the 1990s have people been allowed to think of themselves, once again, as simply Lebanese.

As they struggle to regain their sense of national identity the Lebanese must learn to cope with the trauma of a civil war that left 125,000 dead and 75,000 with permanent disabilities. Over half a million people left the country during the fighting.

Opposite: **An old Druze man and his grand-daughter. The Lebanese are fond of their "family" proverbs, including this one: "If you take your clothes off, you will feel the cold," meaning that those who disregard family members will suffer.**

Left: **Arab families live in a destroyed stadium in southern Beirut.**

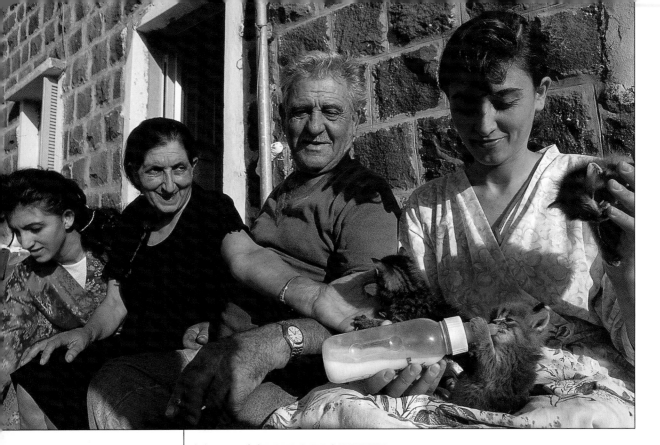

A Christian family in the northern coastal plain.

Over 80% of Lebanese live in urban areas. The last census in Lebanon took place in 1932.

THE ETHNIC MAKEUP

Well over 90% of the population, including Muslims and Christians, are Arabs. In view of the fact that the description "Arab" is sometimes understood to mean "Muslim," not all Lebanese identify themselves primarily as Arabs. Christian Lebanese sometimes prefer to think of themselves as citizens of Lebanon who are Christians, rather than Arabs. The civil war, after all, was largely fought between Christians and Muslims.

In a country that has been torn apart by a civil war for over 15 years, it is not surprising that people have conflicting ideas about how they want to define themselves. Indeed, the whole question of how many Lebanese actually belong to the different religious groups is a highly controversial matter. A census might arrive at a definite set of statistics, but the holding of a census would also remind everyone of the divisions that led to a tragic war within the country. It is mainly for this reason that no modern census has taken place in the country.

The largest ethnic minority are the Armenians, who make up just over 5% of the population. They arrived in the country around the turn of the century to escape massacres in Turkey. In 1924 they were granted citizenship by the French, who wanted to increase the number of Christians in the country. The Armenians have their own language and culture and tend to live together in their own communities in the cities. Like Armenians in other parts of the world, they welcomed the creation of an independent Armenia east of Turkey.

Smaller ethnic minorities are Assyrians, who fled from Iraq in the early decades of the 20th century, and later from Syria in the 1950s. They are all Christians. There is an equally small number of Kurds, about 1% of the population, and being Muslims they have been absorbed into the Arabic culture of the country.

The most important group of non-Lebanese Arabs living in the country are the Palestinians.

Children at a Beirut orphanage dress up for a concert. The girls are wearing headdresses made of cones and veils, similar to those worn by wealthy Lebanese women living in the mountains in the 19th century.

CONFESSIONS

Nearly all Lebanese are Arabs, but they are grouped into what is known within the country as confessions. Confessions are groups based on religion and are the chief means by which Lebanese people identify and define themselves. Indeed, every citizen of Lebanon carries an identity card that states which confession they belong to. It does not necessarily mean that a Christian Lebanese, for example, is a practicing Christian who actually attends church regularly. The confessional categories are more political than religious.

Arab women in their coverall cloaks. The cloak is worn outdoors to shield Muslim women from the sight of males who are not their family members.

ARABS

Lebanon is a predominantly Arab society in terms of both language and culture. A third dimension, that of religion, nearly always contributes to the definition of an Arab society, but Lebanon is an important exception. Nearly all Lebanese speak Arabic as their first language and there is an Arab culture common to the whole country. However, while the Arab world is overwhelmingly Islamic, not all Lebanese are Muslims, and this is very unusual for an Arab society.

Arabs were originally the people who lived in the Arabian peninsula, where Islam was born. As the religion spread, so too did the Arabic language, and the term "Arab" came to mean all those who speak Arabic. Consequently, not all Arabs look the same and the color of their skin and hair varies considerably from light to dark. The Arabs of Lebanon look very much like the Arabs of neighboring Middle Eastern countries, and are usually dark haired with lightly tanned skin.

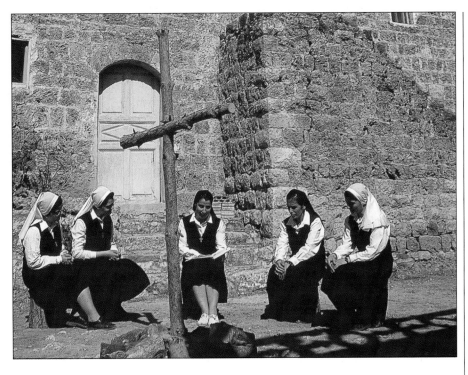

Novices form a prayer group at their convent.

DRUZE

Druze are Muslims and live mostly in the mountainous regions of Lebanon and across the border in parts of southern Syria. In terms of language, dress, and many other aspects of daily culture, Druze are indistinguishable from other Lebanese. It is only their religious beliefs that make them a distinct group of people within the country.

Like all other Muslims, they do not drink alcohol. Druze also refrain from smoking: although smoking is not forbidden to Muslims, it is discouraged.

MARONITES

Most Christians in Lebanon are Maronites, an offshoot of the Catholic Church. They have lived in the country since the fifth century, mostly in the north of Lebanon and in the eastern portion of Beirut. Many Maronites have close links with France and French culture and they speak French fluently.

A Palestinian mother and her child at the Rashidieh Camp in Lebanon. Many Palestinians in Lebanon are not registered, and it is difficult to estimate their numbers.

PALESTINIANS

Palestinians first arrived in 1948 when the state of Israel was created and large numbers were forced to flee north. The international community created the United Nations Relief and Works Committee to look after them, and they were allowed to build camps on the outskirts of Beirut and other large towns. At first, they were registered and entitled to education, health, and other benefits. In the early 1950s this provision came to an end and unregistered refugees who continued to arrive had no legal status whatsoever.

Today, over half the registered Palestinians still live in camps, often with very poor living conditions, and they face disadvantages in nearly all aspects of their life. It is estimated that within the refugee camps there are over 15 different factions and the average Palestinian has no choice but to accept the authority of whatever faction happens to control their area.

During the first half of the civil war, from 1975 to 1982, Palestinians were heavily involved in fighting with the Christian groups. They paid a terrible

price for this in 1976 when some 2,500 Palestinian men, women, and children were murdered by Christian militias in Tel-el-Zaater. More massacres took place in Shatila and Sabra in 1982 under cover of invading Israeli troops.

In the Ain el Helwe Camp in Lebanon, children receive weapons training and practice military discipline. Being prepared for war is a part of their education.

NOWHERE TO RUN TO, NOWHERE TO HIDE

Today, at least 350,000 Palestinians have no hope of citizenship either in Lebanon or in a new Palestinian state. The refugee camps at Shatila and Sabra, where large numbers live, are now facing another disaster. The inhabitants have been attacked and massacred on more than one occasion; the camps were last flattened in 1985 after a long siege by Shiite militias. Both camps have been shelled and rebuilt a number of times.

The camps are now scheduled to be pulled down permanently. The government, as part of its ambitious plan to rebuild Beirut, wishes to construct a new sports stadium on the land occupied by 50,000 Palestinians.

Where will they go? Only some will find a new home overseas or elsewhere in the Middle East. Most are destined to remain in Lebanon.

A familiar military image in Lebanon today is the Syrian Lebanon soldier.

SHAKING OFF THE STEREOTYPE

A familiar image of the Lebanese is that of a young man armed with lethal weapons, sometimes dressed in something resembling a military uniform. Throughout the 1970s and 1980s young men joined the militias that acted as the military wing of different religious power groups. In the mid-1980s, in addition to the armies of Lebanon, Syria, the Palestinians, the United States, France, and the United Nations, there were almost 20 militia groups. With so many players, it was not surprising that outsiders were often confused by the civil war in Lebanon.

The motives that led even boys in their early teens to drop out of school and join the militias were not always clear cut. It was not uncommon for these young men not to know what their militia stood for. What they did see was an economic opportunity (members of militias were paid a regular wage), the offer of protection from rival militias, and a sense of power. These factors often played a more important role than politics. The grim reality was the easy access to arms. Teachers, for example, were sometimes threatened by armed students or militia soldiers.

When the main opposition to the Taif Agreement was defeated in October 1990, the militias were slowly disbanded. Lebanese militias are still found in the south. For most of the country they are a thing of the past and the young men who once manned the checkpoints are now adjusting to peace.

LEBANESE DIASPORA

A diaspora is the spread of an ethnic group beyond the borders of its own territory. There is a long tradition, going back centuries, of Lebanese migrating to other countries.

The earliest generation of Lebanese migrants were mostly male and largely Christian. Many worked as peddlers. Such a job required very hard work but little capital and from such humble beginnings many Lebanese established a successful life far from the eastern Mediterranean. As early as the first decade of the 20th century, it was estimated that over 40% of Lebanon's foreign earnings came from money sent home by Lebanese abroad. The successful emigrant often returns to Lebanon to retire.

Some 20 years ago there were about one million Lebanese living overseas and most of them were Christians. During the civil war, the number of people leaving the country increased, and both Muslims and Christians left. Between 1975 and 1987 well over half a million people, mostly professionals or semiskilled laborers, left the country. At some point during the civil war in Lebanon, nearly one in four Lebanese were living abroad.

People leave Lebanon for primarily economic reasons. They go to a country where there are employment possibilities. In the past the United States was a popular destination, but in recent years the oil-rich states of the Middle East have attracted increasing numbers of Lebanese.

One of the earliest mosques in the United States was built in Ross, North Dakota, by Lebanese emigrants.

Singer and song-writer Paul Anka is Lebanese-American. Well-known Lebanese-Americans include Danny Thomas and Casey Kasem.

LIFESTYLE

LARGE MULTICOLOR BILLBOARDS are a familiar sight along the main roads that lead to and from the capital city's airport. For over a decade the billboards that graced Beirut's airport road carried illustrations of young men blowing up Israeli tanks. Some of them glorified Hizbollah's suicide bombers. In late 1995, however, the government decided that such billboards were giving visitors a negative image of Lebanon that no longer existed. The billboards have been pulled down and more conventional advertisements are beginning to replace them.

Another sign of the new times can be found in the fact that references to "West Beirut" and "East Beirut" are no longer about two halves of a divided city. A Christian storekeeper, when directing a customer to another shop, which may happen to be Muslim-owned, now talks about "another part of town" rather than just "West Beirut."

Left: **Blood seeps from a Star of David, a Jewish symbol, in this Hizbollah poster in South Lebanon.**

Opposite: **A senior citizen of Tripoli sits in an arched passage. Tripoli is the Lebanese city with the most Islamic appearance.**

Many people locked up their homes and left during the civil war in Lebanon. Some of them returned in the early 1990s, after fighting had ended.

STARTING AGAIN

The scene looks peaceful and inviting: green countryside, hills in the distance, the sound of birds in the trees. It is only the ruins of a modern family house and an untended garden that upset the idyllic scene. Part of the house may be occupied if some rooms are safe to inhabit.

All over Lebanon today people are busy rebuilding their homes. A common sight in the countryside is a truck piled with building materials parked outside a partially rebuilt home. Many Lebanese cannot afford to stay in the countryside while they rebuild their dwellings. Beirut offers the best chance of employment and on weekends and during occasional holidays families leave the capital and return to their villages for a working holiday.

In many cases people had to abandon their homes at short notice and only returned months or years later to find the shattered remains. "We were the last to leave. It was the middle of the night, and our neighbors came and knocked on the door, shouting urgently that we had to go; we could hear guns very close. We left with nothing. If we'd been able to take things with us we would have been all right. But we left with nothing and now we've come back with nothing. We thought we'd be gone a few weeks or months. It has been 10 years now." These words of a man from South Lebanon were spoken as he paused before laying some new bricks on the broken wall of his home. When the wall has been repaired he plans to begin work on his garden.

MAKING FRIENDS

A survey conducted shortly after peace was established in 1990 showed that 52% of the Lebanese had their homes completely destroyed, while 27% had homes partially destroyed. As Lebanese families rebuild and repair their homes they are also faced with the more difficult challenge of reestablishing broken relationships with their neighbors.

Many villages once had mixed communities of Christians and Muslims living together. The civil war polarized relationships and neighbors fought neighbors. Friends became enemies overnight. Rebuilding friendships is not always as easy as rebuilding a house because bitter memories remain.

There is, fortunately, a positive side to the hardship caused by the years of fighting. In many instances people joined together to help their neighbors when they all faced the challenge of survival in terribly harsh conditions. In doing this, they were following the age-old custom of neighborly solidarity. The Lebanese have many traditional sayings that reflect the importance of being neighborly, including "Joy is for all, and mourning is for all" and "The neighbor who is near is more important than the brother who is far."

People go on living in bombed out buildings.

63

RICH AND POOR

A major factor affecting the kind of lifestyle available to a Lebanese family is the social inequality between the rich and the poor. In many respects this is no different from most countries in the world.

A survey of the quality of life in one of the refugee camps near Tyre, for example, revealed appalling conditions. Daily rations from United Nations relief funds are the only source of food for many of the refugees. Today in Lebanon, over 50% of all private income is received by one-fifth of the population. The poorest one-fifth of the country, on the other hand, only receive 4%.

Affluence is often open and ostentatious, particularly in the cities. Apartments of the rich are well stocked with appliances, there are many cars on the roads, and children are given music lessons and go to good schools. Before the war, everything the rich could afford was found in the city center, particularly in Beirut: movie theaters, first-class shops, and good schools and colleges. Circling the city were the living quarters of the poor, and the factories where they worked.

The majority of citizens work very hard trying to maintain a decent living on meager

wages constantly threatened by inflation. The upheavals of the last 20 years have accelerated the migration of people from the countryside to Beirut, aggravating the already overcrowded and shortage-ridden existence of the poor.

LIFESTYLE STATISTICS

Population:	Over 3.5 million
Birth rate:	27 births per 1,000 of the population
Death rate:	6 deaths per 1,000 of the population
Life expectancy:	66 years for men; 72 for women
Literacy rate:	80% over the age of 15 can read and write
Unemployment rate:	35%
Occupations:	79% in industry and commerce
	11% in agriculture
	10% in government

Above: **St. George's Bay in Beirut. Thirty years ago the citizens of Beirut had 10 lovely beaches to choose from; today, there are only small private patches of unpolluted beach.**

Opposite: **Few repairs are evident a few years after the end of war, and rubbish clogs open sewers in downtown Beirut.**

ENVIRONMENTAL PROBLEMS

The growing number of people living and working in the city of Beirut has given rise to serious environmental problems. The lack of a public transport system means there is an excessive number of private cars belching out exhaust. Half of the country's 800,000 private cars are in Beirut and air pollution in the city is among the highest in the world.

Highly accelerated projects are being built almost everywhere along the coast. There are few government controls. Building regulations were difficult to enforce during the civil war, and there was little or no control over where and how buildings were constructed. As a result, they were often built too close to one another, with little or no provision for sewage treatment.

Public utilities and services were curtailed during the civil war. As the public supply of electricity is still limited to set periods each day, generators (called motors) are employed. The sound they make is a familiar irritating noise in the towns and they add to the general air pollution. The overall effect of air pollution is sadly visible when looking down from the mountains toward Beirut. There is usually a dense, brown smog.

The Mediterranean Sea, which once provided attractive beaches for holiday makers, is polluted to an unhealthy degree as far as Lebanon is concerned. Over the years garbage has been dumped into the sea by all the countries around the Mediterranean. As a result, the surface water is often covered with small particles of sewage, which sometimes gather into ugly masses of yellow muck. The few patches of unpolluted beach near Beirut that have survived are now the domain of private resorts, which charge for admission.

Deforestation has also taken its toll. Only 3% of the country remains forested, compared with 18% in the 1950s, and the mountain cedars—Lebanon's national emblem—are no longer a common sight.

The shelling of villages and towns resulted in the pollution of the water table and most of the natural springs. People had little choice but to dig makeshift wells, and these too soon became polluted. People living in the refugee camps in Beirut have learned to cope with inadequate sewage facilities and unsafe drinking water.

Above: **Lebanese undergraduate. Women have the right to vote and may participate in politics. Lebanon has three women parliamentarians.**

Opposite: **Older Lebanese women prefer to wear traditional long dresses.**

A WOMAN'S LIFE

In some areas of life the legal system discriminates against women. A man who kills a wife, sister, or mother may avoid conviction if he can prove that the woman committed adultery.

A woman is required by law to obtain her husband's or father's permission for a passport. Only males may confer citizenship on their spouses and children. What this means, in some cases, is that a child may be born stateless if the mother is Lebanese and the father is stateless. The child inherits his father's lack of nationality.

Religious groups have views of a woman's role that may influence their laws concerning marriage and family property rights. Sometimes this means that women are discriminated against. For example, a Sunni inheritance law gives a son twice the share of a daughter. It is also the case that, while a Muslim man may divorce easily, a Muslim woman may do so only with her husband's agreement.

DAILY ROUTINE In rural areas, girls grow up expecting to help in the fields as well as manage all the household chores: washing, cooking, cleaning, and taking care of the children. Their children are likely to have at least 10 years of school, and will grow up expecting greater independence from home. Women in the cities have the same responsibilities, but in urban areas people accept the idea of women working for a salary.

COSMETICS Lebanese women sometimes have colorful red and brown patterns on their hands and feet. The effect is created by applying henna, a dye made from the leaves of the henna shrub. Henna is bought in the form of a powder and mixed with water. It usually comes in two colors—red and black—and these are mixed to provide different shades of red. Sometimes the henna is mixed with yogurt, tea, or coffee, instead of just water; the agent used affects the color. After the dye is applied to the skin, but before it dries, lemon juice is sometimes added to darken the final color from a light orange to a dark red or brown. Fine lines show up more clearly.

Women sometimes use a sugary solution as a waxing lotion. About one cup of sugar is mixed with half a cup of water and a small amount of fresh lemon juice is added. The mixture is boiled to make a concentrated syrup and then left to cool on a cold surface. Before it gets too cold the lotion is applied to the skin as a thin wax.

DRESS What women wear depends on their religion and where they live. Western dress is preferred, and some women are very fashionable. In the countryside, modest long dresses are more in evidence. Outdoors, Muslim women (especially those in rural areas) may wear clothes that cover them from head to toe.

Firewood is used for cooking in rural areas, where cooking is often done outdoors.

RURAL LIFE

Less than one in five Lebanese work in the country—this is a relatively low proportion for the Arab world. In the countryside the extended family has always been the most basic and important form of social organization. As rural folk migrate to towns and cities they bring with them this emphasis on the family network, thus many small businesses in urban areas are run by a small family group.

The majority of farms are very small, less than 5 acres (2 hectares). They are owned by the single family that cultivates the land, and because each farm is so small, the family income usually needs to be supplemented from another source. In the Bekaa Valley the average farm size is around 12 acres (5 hectares), but the lack of rainfall restricts the types of crops that can be grown.

The traditional farmhouse includes a *liwan* ("LEE-wan"), a room that opens on to the outside through a large arched doorway. Such houses are traditionally built of washed earth because it costs too much to cart

building stone in by truck. The flat roof of the house is covered with dried mud. During the hot summer months, the roof inevitably cracks and fractures. Most families have homemade ladders handy to reach the roof and carry out the necessary repairs.

Traditional rural dress for women consists of a loose dress that reaches the ankles, while men wear loose trousers and large shirts. Such loose clothes suit the dry and hot climate.

Women are expected to help in the fields in farming areas. These women are well protected with heavy gloves and sun hats.

HOSPITALITY

A sense of family honor is very important and is expressed in various ways. Hospitality functions as a form of honor and is often extended to include a sense of responsibility for one's guest or visitor. A visitor to a Lebanese home is always treated graciously, and food is naturally offered as an expression of hospitality.

Visitors to the country are often surprised at the hospitality shown them. A social encounter with one friendly person can easily lead to visits from place to place to meet all the family members.

Women and children gather at a pier at the waterfront in Beirut. Group activities are an important part of social life in Lebanon.

VALUES

Sectarianism and the civil war have affected the sense of values held by many Lebanese. The average citizen of the United States has a strong sense of being an American. For many Lebanese, loyalty to family and religion is felt just as strongly as a sense of nationality. In a country that has been shattered by years of prolonged civil conflict, family solidarity has become the only reliable source of stability. For example, an extended family network will collaborate to finance the education of a young person, and because there is no social security system, the family becomes an essential means of caring for the ill and the elderly.

Honor is highly valued and is often more important than income. Among males, there is a macho element that is not very different from its counterpart in other cultures. It features a keen regard for male prowess and calls for vengeance to address a perceived insult.

CHRISTIAN SCHOOLS

Jesuits (members of a Catholic religious order) arrived in 1625 and with the Maronites they established the first schools in Lebanon. In 1820 American Presbyterian missionaries landed in Beirut and in 1866 they established what was to become the American University of Beirut. Protestant rivalry with Catholicism led to other schools being established by Jesuits.

These schools taught in Arabic and revived the study of Arabic literature. The achievements of Arab civilization in the past were studied and, aided by Western notions of democracy, helped to fuel demands for political freedom from Ottoman rule.

The American University of Beirut, founded in 1866 as the Syrian Protestant College, provides education for all, regardless of religion. In this respect it is different from the French University of Saint Joseph, also in Beirut, which caters more to Christians.

EDUCATION

The most noticeable difference between schools in Lebanon and those in Western countries such as the United States is the high percentage of private schools in Lebanon. Only primary education is provided free of charge by the government, and even then it is not compulsory. Nearly all the secondary schools are funded by private religious groups. Parents who can afford to send their children to private secondary schools will also pay for a private primary education. Many Lebanese children would receive no education at all if it were not for the privately funded Islamic schools. The prevalence of religious schools does, unfortunately, make it difficult to break down the religious divisions that have separated the Lebanese for so long.

Despite the lack of government-funded schools, the overall literacy rate remains one of the highest in the Middle East. Young people, however, have been the victims of the years of fighting, and one in five Lebanese under the age of 20 is illiterate.

The school year runs from October to June. In many private schools the lessons are taught in French or English, although all the students speak and use Arabic outside the classroom.

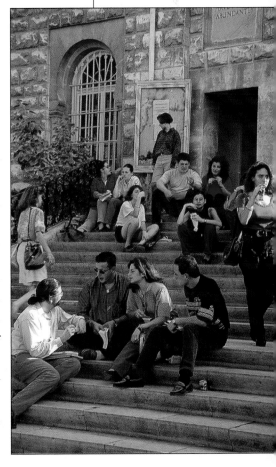

RELIGION

ABOUT 70% OF ALL LEBANESE are Muslims, and there are five legally recognized Islamic groups. Of these, the Druze, Shiite, and Sunni are the most important groups in Lebanon.

Christians make up the remaining 30% of the population, and more than half of them are Catholic. There are 11 legally recognized Christian sects. Minority Christian groups include the Nestorian Assyrians, who arrived in Lebanon after the massacre of their people in Iraq in 1933. Non-Christian minorities include Baha'is and Jews.

In all, there are over 20 different religious sects spanning Islam and Christianity in Lebanon. The way each group defines itself and its relationships with other religious groups is known in Lebanon as confessionalism. The more usual word to describe this kind of social organization is sectarianism.

Opposite: **Oblivious to her hard seat, a Palestinian woman reads her prayer book.**

Left: **The archbishop and members of the Greek Orthodox Church leaving their church in Beirut. The Greek Orthodox Church in Lebanon is affiliated to that in Damascus, Syria.**

ISLAM

The Islamic faith originated in Arabia in the seventh century through the Prophet Mohammed. Followers of Islam are known as Muslims and their religion is a comprehensive one, covering nearly every aspect of life.

The religion is based on the observance of five pillars: the creed, the performance of prayer, the giving of alms, the observance of fasting, and the performance of a pilgrimage to Mecca.

THE CREED The Islamic creed is summed up in the words: "There is no God but God and Mohammed is the Prophet of God." The Islamic faith includes a belief in angels as messengers of God, in prophets who receive messages from God, and in holy books that express these messages. Muslims also believe in a last day of judgment that will be announced by the archangel Asrafil blowing on a trumpet. After judgment all people will go to either paradise or hell.

The Koran, the holy book of Islam, gives the names of 28 prophets, of whom Mohammed was the last. Twenty-one of the prophets are also mentioned in the Bible, including Jesus. Unlike Christianity, where Jesus is given divinity as the son of God, in Islam Jesus is just one of the prophets. The scriptures of Abraham, the Torah of Moses, the Psalms of David, and the Gospels of the New Testament are also believed to be prophetic revelations of God.

PRAYER Islam calls for a Muslim to pray at least five times a day: at sunrise, noon, late afternoon, sunset, and night. Worshipers are called to prayer by a mosque official, the *muezzin* ("moo-EZ-in"), traditionally from the top of the minaret of a mosque. These days, the calls are usually a recording broadcast from an amplifier.

There are some fascinating overlaps between Islam and Christianity in Lebanon. Worshipers from both religions esteem the Virgin Mary, and texts that predate Christianity by over 2,000 years mention a Virgin Lady. The Virgin of Lebanon and the Lady of Lebanon are mentioned in the texts from Ugarit that date from around 1400 B.C

Muslims can pray in a mosque, but this is not obligatory or always practical. Some public buildings have a small room reserved for prayers. Friday is the most holy day of the week, akin to the Christian Sunday, and on this day Muslim men will try to attend a mosque for their prayers. Women usually pray at home, but those who choose to pray at the mosque will do so in a section set aside for them.

Prayers begin by a ritual washing of the body to show one's willingness to be purified. Physical contact with a member of the other sex is not permitted until after prayers, and if a Muslim man accidentally touches a woman, he must wash himself ritually once again before praying.

The worshiper always prays in the direction of Mecca and a prescribed cycle of prayers is made. Prayers usually consist of passages from the Koran. Worshipers prostrate themselves in a series of different positions for each of the five daily prayers. A prayer mat is used for this purpose.

Muslim women learn to read the Koran in a mosque. Knowledge of Arabic is a prerequisite, and there is no age limit to start the process.

Images of Muslim leaders in the interior of a mosque in Marakeh, southern Lebanon.

GIVING ALMS Muslims who earn a certain minimum salary must donate 2.5% of their annual income to the poor. Muslims also pay a contribution during the fasting month of Ramadan, and even newborns are not exempted from this contribution. The religious authority appoints mosque officials to make this collection annually at the appropriate time. The amount may vary every year, since it is tagged to the price of staple foods.

FASTING Fasting takes place during the month of Ramadan when no food or drink is consumed between sunrise and sunset. Among the other prohibitions are smoking during the fasting hours and thinking or speaking ill of others. Only those who are ill or very young are exempted from the fast. Muslim children are trained to fast from the age of 7, when they usually fast for half a day. By about the age of 9 or 10, they are ready for full-day fasts. Every night during Ramadan, in the mosque or at home, Muslims go through the ritual of a special prayer in addition to the evening prayer.

PILGRIMAGE TO MECCA The pilgrimage to Mecca is something all Muslims who can afford it do at least once in their life. The traditional

THE SIXTH PILLAR OF ISLAM

The sixth pillar of Islam is *jihad* ("JEE-hahd"), which translates as "striving in the way of God." It is a much misunderstood term that is open to more than one interpretation. Consequently, its meaning has been disputed and argued about within the Islamic community.

It is often rendered in English as "holy war." *Jihad* can mean a holy war against the godless, but it also applies to a holy war by an individual against one's own unholy instincts. In this latter sense it has some similarity with the Christian idea of an individual striving to be good and struggling with his own conscience.

month for the big pilgrimage is the last month of the Islamic calendar. (Smaller pilgrimages can be made at any time of the year.) The pilgrimage leads to the forgiving of a Muslim's past sins.

Muslims make careful preparations for their pilgrimage, some as early as a year prior to leaving. Clearing all financial obligations and making sure their family members have been provided for are religious requirements. Special classes conducted by religious teachers coach would-be pilgrims in the rites, prayers, and rules. Muslim men buy seamless clothes.

The Taynal Mosque in Tripoli features more elaborate decor than is usually seen inside a mosque.

SHIITES

Shiism ("SHEE-iz-uhm") is a religious movement that traces its descent back to the murder of Ali, the son-in-law and nephew of the Prophet Mohammed. Supporters of Ali who supported his claim to be the leader after Mohammed became known as *Shi'i* (followers of Ali). This is usually anglicized as Shiites ("SHE-ites").

A Druze man at the waterfront. He is dressed in traditional Lebanese pants that are loose from the waist to the knee and tight below the knee.

The most important Shiite group is the "Twelver" Shiites, who believe that there were 12 holy men after Mohammed—Ali and his descendants—who did not die and will return in triumph one day as the saviors of the world.

In Lebanon today the Shiites tend to be the poorer citizens of the country and mostly share a farming background.

DRUZE

Druze are an Islamic group that emerged in the 11th century as a branch of the Shiite sect. Shiite Islam has always been more mystical than the mainstream Sunni religion, and this mysticism is found among the Druze. The Druze believe in reincarnation. Druze Muslims do not seek or accept converts. They believe in protecting the secrets of their religion and will worship as mainstream Muslims when in a non-Druze Muslim community or as Christians when in a Christian community.

Druze believe that God has taken various incarnations as a living person on earth, including that of Jesus Christ, and that he last took human form as al-Hakim in the 11th

century. The name of the religion is thought to derive from al-Darazi, a follower of al-Hakim.

Today, the Druze make up the country's majority religion, and about one in three Lebanese are Druze Muslims. As a general rule they only marry among themselves. They do not worship in a mosque but meet for prayers on a Thursday evening in a house close to their village.

SUNNI MUSLIMS

Sunni is a mainstream sect of Islam found throughout the Middle East and 80% of all Muslims in the world are Sunnis. They do not accept the Shiite view about Mohammed's successor, and because Sunnis form the majority, their view is the orthodox one.

In Lebanon the Sunnis are traditionally associated with the coastal cities of Beirut, Tripoli, and Sidon. Most of the Palestinian refugees in Lebanon are also Sunnis.

A Muslim group on an outing. The man wears a *kaffiyeh*, an Arab head-dress that is adopted by some men in Lebanon, while the women adhere to the Muslim custom of wearing ankle-length dresses.

CATHOLICS

The most important Christian groups in Lebanon are Uniate Catholics, which means the members accept the authority of the Pope in Rome but practice their own particular rites. They include the Maronites, Greek Catholics, and Armenian Catholics.

The Greek Catholics are also called Melchites. They are the descendants of a Greek Orthodox community that broke off from the Greek Orthodox Church in the 18th century. They retain many of their Greek rites but accept the authority of the Pope in Rome.

The Armenian Catholics are distinguished by using their own language in their religious ceremonies. They came to Lebanon to escape massacres of Armenians by the Turks around World War I.

The interior of a Catholic church in Lebanon.

THE MARONITE CHURCH

The Maronites are Catholics who are traditionally associated with the northern part of the country, although they also live in southern Lebanon. They originated in Syria in the early seventh century and shortly after moved into Lebanon. They take their name from St. Maro, a fourth century monk. Originally the Maronites were monothelite, believing that Christ has one will but two natures, but in the 12th century they grew closer to mainstream Roman Catholicism. They elect their own church leader, a patriarch, through their bishops, and if the bishops cannot agree within 15 days, the Pope in Rome makes an appointment.

Catholic weddings are solemnized in church.

In 1736 the Maronites became affiliated with the Catholic Church, and this provided Catholic France with an excuse to ally itself with them in Lebanon. The Turkish government retaliated by supporting and encouraging the heretical Muslim group, the Druze, as a counterweight to France's influence. Today the number of Maronites in Lebanon is approaching 250,000. Traditionally, Maronites have identified themselves with the West, as they did in the time of the Crusades.

CHURCHES AND MOSQUES

The history of religion in Lebanon can be seen in its architecture. The Grand Mosque of Umar in Beirut has foundation stones from the Roman and Byzantine eras when the building was a Christian church. It was a Christian cathedral during the Crusades. In the 13th century it was converted into a mosque. The Great Mosque in Tripoli has a similar history. It dates from the 14th century but incorporates parts of an earlier Christian cathedral of St. Mary of the Tower. The Italian-style minaret of the mosque is believed to be the original bell-tower of the cathedral.

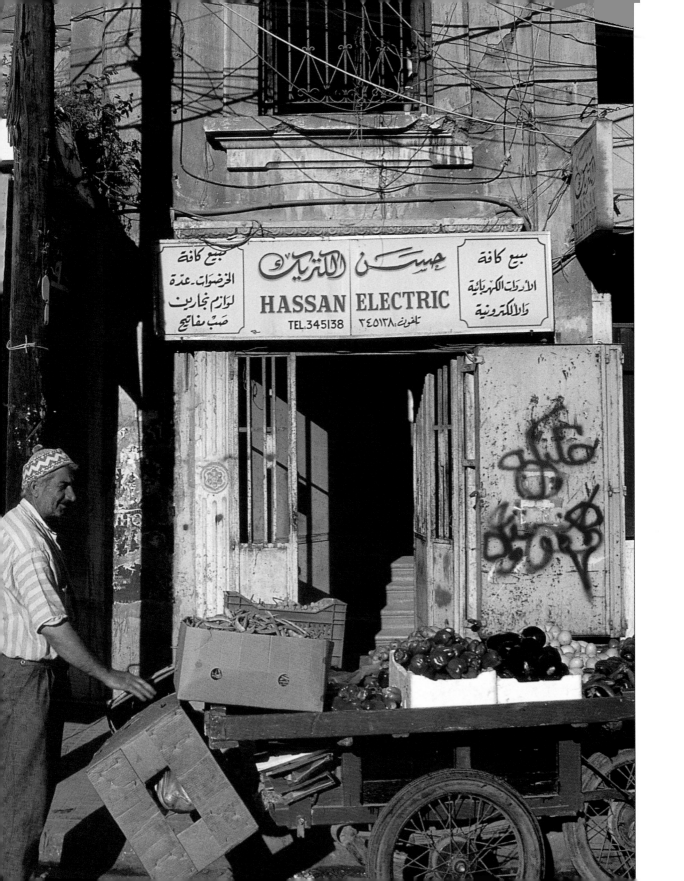

LANGUAGE

NEARLY ALL LEBANESE speak and write Arabic. The most important second languages are French and English. English is more important than French for international business, but the legacy of French rule in Lebanon has ensured that French is often more commonly spoken than English.

The most important minority language is Armenian, spoken by the relatively small number of Armenians who arrived in Lebanon around the time of World War I.

ARABIC

Arabic, the everyday language for nearly all Lebanese, is spoken by over 150 million people around the world. As the name suggests, it was originally the language of Arabia, and as Islam spread beyond Arabia in the seventh and eighth centuries so did the language of the religion.

Left and opposite: **Arabic is the official language in Lebanon, but French and English are used widely.**

Arabic has more than one form. The spoken form, as used by people in their everyday life, is known as colloquial Arabic. The various Arabic-speaking countries have their own forms of colloquial Arabic. A Lebanese speaks Arabic and so does an Egyptian, for example, but their Arabic is not identical and the speakers cannot always easily communicate.

Classical Arabic is quite different. It is the language of the Koran and provides a common and shared written form for all Arab speakers.

A third form of Arabic is a mixture of the first two. In its spoken form it provides a shared language for all Lebanese. In the more remote mountainous regions in the eastern part of the country there are local dialects that lack a written form. These are only used for communication within the local group and thus are used in a geographically small area.

Arabic belongs to the diglossic languages, or languages with significant differences between spoken and written forms. Arabic is regarded as a difficult diglossic language, and recent attempts have been made to modernize it. Lebanese linguists have worked on the compilation of a Lebanese dictionary, one that lists words by theme rather than in the traditional ordering system of Arabic that groups words according to their linguistic roots.

ENDANGERED DOCUMENTS

The Sherfe monastery on the hills north of Beirut has the world's sixth-largest library of manuscripts. Its collection of over 3,000 manuscripts, dating from the 11th to the 19th centuries, is considered the most important in the world after the collections of the British Museum, the Vatican, and the national libraries in Paris, Berlin, and St. Petersburg.

The collection in the Sherfe monastery includes the diary that Michael the Syriac kept during the 11th century to chronicle Crusaders' expeditions in the Middle East. Unfortunately, due to atmospheric conditions and the activity of insects, priceless documents like this diary are disintegrating. The diary and other ancient documents are kept in glass cabinets in two dark rooms of the ancient monastery and are now too fragile to be consulted or even touched.

Some of the manuscripts were written in Syriac, an ancient language related to Aramaic and considered to be the dialect spoken by Christ. Syriac scholars also wrote in Arabic, and between the 8th and 13th centuries they translated into Arabic the works of Aristotle and Plato. The texts in Arabic went to Spain (when the Arabs controlled Spain), where they were translated into Latin, thus providing a cultural foundation for the European Renaissance.

The Sherfe library was established in 1780 by the founder of the monastery, Monsignor Ignace Michel III Jarwa. Some of his monks were assigned the task of tracking down original manuscripts that lay scattered around the eastern lands of the Ottoman empire. They were given funds to purchase manuscripts and, when a sale could not be arranged, had the task of copying the entire manuscript so that a copy could be preserved in the monastery library. Without the work of the monks from the Sherfe monastery, many important documents would have been lost forever.

Arabic became established as the chief language of Lebanon under the Abbasid dynasty (750–1258).

With the civil war behind them, the Lebanese are more concerned today with getting ahead. Since English is perceived as the language of the business world, Lebanese parents are now pushing their children to take English-language classes.

THE POLITICS OF LANGUAGE

Language is more than just a means of communication in Lebanon. A person's choice of language has a symbolic importance that is usually related to politics. For example, some Christians use French rather than Arabic to signal their political opposition to Muslim groups.

Some Maronite groups would prefer schools to adopt the Lebanese colloquial dialect of Arabic instead of teaching classical Arabic. Those who have little sympathy for Arab nationalism perceive the use of classical Arabic as a tool of Arab nationalism. If Lebanon was to adopt its colloquial form of Arabic as the national language it would be distancing itself from the rest of the Arab world. This is very unlikely to happen.

Even names tend to signify one's religion in Lebanon. Popular Muslim names are Mohammed and Ahmad, while French names like Pierre and Michel are likely to be chosen by Christians. Biblical names like Sarah may belong to either a Christian or a Muslim.

A ROSE BY ANY OTHER NAME

It is very usual for Arabic words, when transliterated into English, to have more than one spelling. The Arabic musical instrument from which the European lute is derived appears in writing as both the *'ud* and the *oud*, both pronounced in the same way ("OOD"). Another example is the Muslim sect known as both the Druze and the Druse.

Transliteration from Arabic to English is difficult for two reasons: there are sounds in Arabic with no equivalent in English, and there are vowel sounds in Arabic that do not appear in written Arabic. Due to the fact that there is no agreed system for transliteration, words regularly appear with different spellings.

BODY LANGUAGE

Gesticulations form a part of conversations all over the world, whatever the language, but they vary from one culture to another. The common gesticulations found in Lebanon are fairly typical of the Middle East as a whole. People may express a simple negative, "no," by raising the eyebrows and lifting the head up and back a little. The gesture is often accompanied by a "tsk tsk" noise. In some parts of the world this noise usually expresses disapproval, but it carries no suggestion of a snub in the Middle East.

Shaking the head from side to side does not mean "no," but "I do not understand." Stretching out a hand as if to open a door, while at the same time flicking the wrist and hand, can mean "what is the problem?" or "what do you want?" It often functions as a general expression of enquiry.

The right hand held over the heart usually means "no thank you." A traditional female greeting in Lebanon is raising the right hand and lightly touching one's chest. It is an Islamic gesture. In most social intercourse the right hand is used to give or receive anything.

Men hold hands as a gesture of friendship or simply companionship. A male stranger asking for directions may be taken by the hand and shown the right direction.

In conversation, urban Lebanese switch easily from Arabic to English to French, and they use hand gestures freely.

ARTS

LEBANON HAS A TRADITION in the arts that is as ancient as its monuments. Lebanese literature has been translated and widely disseminated, and the works of some Lebanese writers such as Kahlil Gibran are familiar to readers around the world. Before the civil war, the art scene in Lebanon, particularly in traditional music and dance, was the talk of the Middle East, and the international festival in Baalbek was world famous.

ANCIENT ART

Lebanon is justly proud of the many architectural and other artistic remains that make up its most celebrated artistic heritage. The National Museum in Beirut has an especially rich collection of ancient art, dating back to terra cotta figures of 3000 B.C. There are also Phoenician figures, dated to around 1600 B.C. Adornments on many of these figures—such as the way hair is plaited or the rich array of bracelets—reveal the influence of Egypt. Phoenician jewelry also shows the influence of Egyptian art, including the preference for amethyst, a violet-to-purple form of quartz.

Above: **Lebanon is fortunate in possessing good examples of art from historic periods, such as this hunting scene carved in stone from Baalbek.**

Opposite: **Among the traditional crafts practiced in Lebanon is that of engraving. The artisan here is a 12-year-old boy from the village of Kalamoun near Tripoli.**

One of the most highly regarded objects in the National Museum is an 11th century B.C. hand-carved sarcophagus made for the king of Byblos. The king is shown enthroned between two sphinxes, a mythological monster with a human head and a lion's body, holding a lotus blossom. The sphinx originated in the East, probably in Egypt, and is commonly found in ancient art from the eastern Mediterranean region. What really makes the sarcophagus outstanding is a carved alphabetic inscription that is one of the very earliest appearances of writing in the world.

The Palace at Beit-ed-Din, some 30 miles (50 km) from Beirut, is the best example of 19th century Lebanese architecture to be found anywhere in the country. It was built for the Emir Beshir, who governed Lebanon for 50 years, and its construction took 30 years.

The palace is filled with porticoed courts, arcades, and fountains. The ceilings and walls were richly decorated by the best craftsmen in the country, using tiny pieces of mirror to create intricate designs in glass.

BAALBEK Baalbek is a small town in the Bekaa Valley, near the Anti-Lebanon mountains. It was known in the past as Heliopolis (not to be confused with the Heliopolis of ancient Egypt), but is now world-famous for its imposing Greco-Roman ruins, including a temple to the ancient Greek god, Dionysus (called Bacchus by the Romans). In the seventh century Arabs turned Baalbek into a military base and built over many of the existing ruins. Paradoxically, this helped to preserve the archeological remains by keeping them a secret for a very long time.

The entrance and front courtyard of the Beit-ed-Din, home of Beshir Shihab II. The Shihab family's regime was harsh, and the people revolted. The emir was forced to leave Lebanon in 1840.

The temple has magnificent stately columns built from gigantic blocks of locally quarried stone, measuring 62 by 14 by 11 feet (19 by 4 by 3 meters). The builders of Baalbek also used pillars of rose granite imported from Egypt, and it has been estimated that it took some three years for the granite to be transported and erected at Baalbek.

Delicate sculptures in Baalbek depict lines of twining vines and other plants including poppies and wheat. There is a sculpture of the Greek sun god, Helios, which gave the town its earlier name of Heliopolis ("city of the Sun").

EXCAVATING ART The multibillion-dollar rebuilding of Beirut has unearthed ancient art and artifacts going back to Phoenician times, some 2,500 years ago. The work done by archeologists is painstaking and slow.

They may use toothbrushes to unearth evidence of a Phoenician neighborhood, while nearby, bulldozers are used in the laying of sewer pipes and electrical cables for the new Beirut.

The Phoenician neighborhood being excavated includes six houses where fishermen once lived, and the narrow roads and arches that they used are still intact in places. Over the top of this Phoenician settlement the Ottomans also built homes. A stretch of Ottoman wall 200 feet (60 meters) long is among the archeological finds, along with tombs, kilns for glass and pottery production, and mosaic floors from the Roman-Byzantine period.

The excavation work has also unearthed a treasure trove of antiquities from ancient Roman times: statues, glassware, and a whole stretch of road still bearing the marks made by chariot wheels. An inscription on a mosaic has been discovered with the following advice: "Jealousy is the worst of all evils, the only good about it is that it eats up the eyes and heart of the jealous."

Archeological investigations in Lebanon have unearthed valuable facts about its ancient cities. One of these is that the port of Byblos has been continuously inhabited for about 5,000 years.

An *'ud* maker tests his instrument.

MUSICAL INSTRUMENTS

Traditional instruments include a flute-like instrument called the *nay* ("NAY"), which is found in many Middle Eastern cultures as well as in North Africa. It is a relatively difficult instrument to play, especially when compared to the recorder that it resembles. Only the more talented musician can actually play the entire three-octave range of the nay. It is more common for musicians to use nays of different sizes to cover the three octaves.

Traditional musicians also play a drum called the *daff* ("DAHF"), which resembles a tambourine. Another tambourine-like instrument is the *riq* ("reek").

The musical instrument with the most ancient lineage is the *'ud*. It dates back to at least the seventh century and is regarded as the forerunner of the European lute. The *'ud* is the most important musical instrument in Arab culture and there are a number of slightly different types. It is played with a plectum or with the fingers of both hands.

A NEW MUSIC FOR NEW TIMES

Lebanon has a tradition of folk music, and children are taught traditional music from their first year in school. However, new music that combines Arabic and Western arrangements is gaining ground.

When car bombs and kidnappings were regular events in Beirut, the lyrics of musician Marcel Khalife reflected this highly charged political atmosphere. He wrote songs that dealt with experiences common for many Lebanese—being interrogated by border guards, for example. His music was regarded with suspicion by many of those in positions of political power. To the ordinary people of war-torn Lebanon, however, he was a folk hero who raised despair into poetry and reduced his audiences to tears.

Now that peace has been achieved, Khalife has given up songwriting and concentrates on instrumental compositions. "Now that things are

Any social occasion for the family is one for impromptu music and dancing.

Above: **Lebanon's national dance is the** *dabke,* **a lively dance performed by a group. In prearranged performances, dancers wear the traditional dress of people living in the mountains.**

Opposite: **What most people know as belly dancing calls for skillful hip movement.**

changing, words are not important," he said before an audience in Washington D.C. at the start of a 12-city U.S. tour.

His album *Jadal* is a concerto for two performed with the *riq* and a bass guitar. Khalife has also composed works for philharmonic orchestras, citing 13th century Arab historians who wrote of ensembles of up to 100 musicians. His favorite instrument is the *'ud.*

A Lebanese singer, Rabih El-Khawli, is famous among Arabic-speaking people around the world because he gives concerts in France, England, Australia, Sweden, Africa, and throughout North and South America. He started his singing career at a show called Studio Elfan in 1980. Since then his popularity has spread to Syria, Jordan, Palestine, Iraq, Saudi Arabia, and the entire Gulf region. He is also very popular in countries like Algeria, Tunisia, Morocco, Libya, and Egypt.

DANCE

The national dance is the *dabke* ("DAHB-key"), a very energetic folk dance originating in the Bekaa Valley and South Lebanon. Nowadays, it is performed throughout the country. It is a living dance, not one preserved for tourists and special cultural shows, and amateur groups are often seen practicing the steps. The Lebanese dance the *dabke* to celebrate their enjoyment of life at any occasion where people gather, from simple family parties to feasts.

Performances of the *dabke* provide an increasingly rare opportunity to see people wearing traditional Lebanese mountain dress. The dance is performed by women wearing kerchiefs and brightly colored skirts. The traditional music that accompanies the dance has a distinctive sound: jaunty but also haunting.

The *dabke* has a number of themes that allow for variations in the dance form. They usually relate to aspects of village life such as marriage and disputes over land. The dance was traditionally performed by villagers when the day's work was done.

Belly dancing, involving sinuous and sometimes vigorous movements of the hips and abdomen, is often seen performed by young women, both informally and at nightclubs.

FOLK ART

Many of the folk arts practiced in Lebanon are a mixture of those characteristic of the Levant and the larger Arab world.

In carpet weaving, a well-established craft, the necessary skills and knowledge of traditional motifs are passed down from one generation to another within a family. The motifs and patterns for carpets reveal the influence of the Islamic world, being mainly nonfigurative and favoring abstract but colorful designs.

Filigree ornamental work in fine gold wire is a speciality, an offshoot of the jewelry craft that Lebanon is famous for. The motifs found in jewelry designs betray a strong Turkish influence from the Ottoman period. Flowers, birds, and crescents made of semiprecious stones and diamonds are favorite designs.

Artisans who work with precious metals used to do their toolwork outside their shops in the bazaar, or souk. Lumps of gold were "pulled" by two or three men by fixing the gold to another man's belt and stretching the gold out as the man with the belt slowly turned in circles.

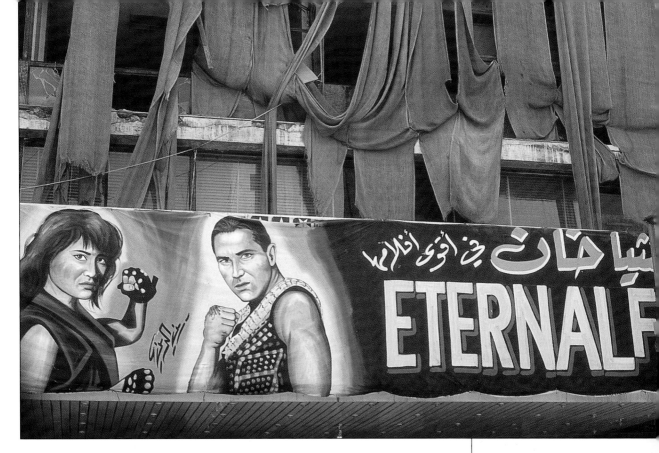

Work in gold and metal inlay work are the province of Lebanese men. Women, usually those living in the countryside, tend to specialize in embroidery work in linen, cotton, and lace.

Movie-going is a national pastime. It's business as usual for the cinema on Rue Hamra in Beirut, regardless of the curtains from the derelict apartments above.

CINEMA

Eloquent testimony to the resilience of Lebanese culture is found in the intelligent, sensitive films that continued to be made throughout the civil war. A good example is *The Encounter*, directed by Burham 'Alawiyya, a film based on the trials of two victims of religious and political divisions in their country. The man, a Shiite Muslim from the south, and his girlfriend, a Christian who lives in the east, communicate by telephone, but their plans to meet are frustrated by the war. They resort to exchanging cassette tapes to maintain their friendship, but when a real opportunity presents itself for a face-to-face encounter they both avoid it because of a mutual realization that the war has changed their relationship.

In 1991 the Cannes Film Festival prize was awarded to Lebanese movie director Maroun Bagdadi for *Hors de Vie* (*Out of Life*).

99

Newspaper and book publishing began in the late 19th century and is linked to the establishment of universities by Christian missionaries in that period.

LITERATURE

The leading international novelist in the Middle East today is the Lebanese writer Hanan Al-Shaykh. Her works have been translated into English, including her most recent novel *Beirut Blues*. A more recently published Lebanese writer who has also been translated into English is Huda Barakat; her first novel is *The Stone of Laughter*.

Neither Al-Shaykh nor Barakat can escape the impact of the civil war that tore apart their country for so long. But neither is concerned in their writing to examine the conflicting loyalties that drove their countrymen to kill each other. Politics, in the narrow sense of religious and nationalist causes, is of less interest to the novelists than the human landscape revealed by the war. Barakat's novel is especially concerned with matters of gender. *The Stone of Laughter* has a male central character who, as the war proceeds, is sucked into a masculine world that eventually leads him to reject the feminine.

Nour Salman is a Lebanese poet who reflects on the bitter legacy of 17 years of civil unrest that witnessed the breakdown of community life. During periods of intense fighting in the cities, the people of Beirut were always aware of the dangers of falling victim to the fighting. They felt like hostages in their own city so that, as Salman expressed it, "We are the inhabitants of the cages."

Other important Lebanese writers include the poet Khalil Gibran, the novelist Amin Malouf, and playwright Elias Khoury.

ZAJAL A literary folk tradition, *zajal* ("TSAH-zahl"), is a form of poetry involving a group of poets who take part in a witty dialogue by improvising lines of verse. It is usually sung rather than recited and often forms part of a village festival, being performed while people eat and drink.

A museum in Bsharri is dedicated to Kahlil Gibran, the Lebanese mystic, poet, and artist who was born there. His best-known book is *The Prophet* (1923). He also wrote *The Forerunner: His Parables and Poems* (1920) and *Sand and Foam: A Book of Aphorisms.* Kahlil Gibran lived in New York city and Boston in the early 20th century.

BEIRUT BLUES

Hanan Al-Shaykh's novel, *Beirut Blues*, takes the form of a series of 10 letters written to friends and public figures by the central female character, Asmahan. The background to all the letters is the civil war, which is described as raging in the "demons' playground" of Lebanon but drawing to an end as it "dies of weariness."

One of the letters in the novel is written to Asmahan's idol, American blues and jazz singer Billie Holiday. The blues is a music of lament, sad but resilient, and a comparison is made between Holiday and a Lebanese singer, Ruhiyya. The American singer "heard the blues played again and again on records rising and falling and spinning like globes in circular seas," while Ruhiyya "heard them from minarets and in the songs of the Shia [Shiite] martyr's passion plays." The singers are seen to have something important in common, and West meets East in a cultural duet: "Neither of you resorted to the pen. ... instead you both sing the reality you live."

PRIZE WINNER

Amin Malouf is a Lebanese writer who left his country to live and work in France in 1976. Seventeen years later, in 1993, he won the Priz Goncourt, France's most prestigious literary award. He received the prize for his novel *The Rock of Tanios*, a love story set in early 19th century Lebanon.

The winner of the Priz Goncourt receives the princely sum of 50 francs—less than $10—but the prize carries the assurance of international renown and attention, as well as increased sales of the book.

LEISURE

SOCIAL LIFE AND LEISURE TIME in Lebanon is primarily based around the family. This does not mean, however, that Lebanese people like to keep just to themselves and their close family members. Socializing with others is very important and enjoyable to most Lebanese and is usually accompanied by a degree of hospitality not commonly found in the West.

THE FAMILY

Many Lebanese homes are based around the extended family, with grandparents often living with one of their children and his or her family. Other married children and their families join this extended family on festive and holiday occasions, considerably enlarging the family group.

Partly due to the disruption caused by the years of fighting, and partly because Lebanese people have a long tradition of traveling abroad for work and study, family reunions are often organized whenever there is a holiday or free time available. In recent years there has also been a continuous migration of people from the countryside to Beirut and other large towns; this has caused many families to be separated. When there is a holiday, families wish to be reunited and this becomes an important leisure activity for many Lebanese people.

Opposite: **Comfortably seated in her courtyard, a Lebanese woman prepares food while enjoying the company of her friend, who busies herself with embroidery.**

Below: **In Junia, two women bask in the sun by a pool.**

Two men enjoy a game of cards and their water pipes.

SOCIALIZING

Spending part of the day with an acquaintance or two and whiling away the time in casual conversation is a popular leisure activity. The scene shown above is sometimes used in tourist literature to represent a typical aspect of the country's culture: men sitting in a café sipping tea or coffee, or perhaps sucking on a nargileh (water pipe), and chatting while playing a game of cards or backgammon. Every town has at least one café where men of all ages meet to socialize. Women do not usually visit cafés; their socializing is more likely to take place in the home.

A NIGHT OUT

Young Lebanese people enjoy American and French music, as well as movies from the United States and France. The movies are usually shown screened in their original language with subtitles in Arabic.

In the past, Beirut was famous for its active and cosmopolitan nightlife. Now that the war is over and normality is beginning to return, many dance clubs and bars have reopened in the capital.

THE IMPORTANCE OF CIVILITY

Civility has been refined to an art in Lebanon. When people meet one another to socialize, even in an informal situation, they often begin the encounter with a number of greetings. Mutual enquiries about health are also exchanged. This may not seem very different from social encounters in the West, but in practice it is more prolonged and formal. Various greetings are made and there is a reciprocal response to each, with slight variations in the greetings and the responses according to the gender of the participants. This reflects the importance attached to civility in Middle East culture.

A common exchange begins with *salaam alaykum* ("sah-LAHM ah-LIE-koom"), which means "peace be with you." The usual reponse is *wa alaykum as-salaam* ("wah a-LIE-koom ah-sah-LAHM"), or "and upon you be peace."

The importance of friends and family is stressed in Lebanese proverbs. But it is true that in Lebanon, as elsewhere, it is the old who retain the traditional sayings. The young prefer to pursue modern ideas, and their tastes are similar to those of Western youths.

A soccer ball, an empty alley, and a group of spectators—all that is needed for a game.

SPORTS

Soccer is the most popular sport; it is usually called football. The game is played in urban areas as well as in the countryside. Basketball is becoming increasingly popular in Beirut and other large towns. Playgrounds and school yards often have basketball courts. Ping-pong is also popular. Swimming and water sports such as boating and water-skiing are popular in the warmer months. The health-conscious in Beirut who have little time to holiday in resorts or no money for private clubs can be seen jogging down the Corniche, a long beachfront walk popular with anglers and strolling families.

SKIING The six ski resorts in the mountains of Lebanon come alive with skiers between December and April each year when heavy snows cover the mountains. Lebanon's best-known ski resort is at the Cedars in the north where there is a grove of the famous trees.

Skiing was introduced to Lebanon by a Lebanese engineer who studied in Switzerland and returned home in 1913. He was so enthusiastic about the sport he had enjoyed in Switzerland that he set about introducing it to his fellow countrymen. But skiing only took off when the French army later opened a skiing school to train men to patrol the mountainous areas, which were not otherwise easily accessible in the winter.

Between 1948 and 1994 Lebanon sent skiers to every Winter Olympics. In 1994, however, new Olympic regulations disqualified smaller countries like Lebanon from participating. This has not diminished the appeal of the sport in the country. On a fine Sunday it is not uncommon for 10,000 skiers to take to the slopes.

TRADITIONAL GAMES

These days many Lebanese spend their leisure time watching television. Family members also enjoy board games, and men are particularly fond of backgammon, which they call *tawleh*, after the table designed specially for the game.

Chess and card games are also popular. Men can often be observed outdoors, playing one of these games and enjoying each other's company.

FESTIVALS

THE MOST IMPORTANT FESTIVALS in Lebanon are religious. With both Muslim and Christian communities, there are festivals most months of the year.

Opposite: **Music, cultural dances, and splendid costumes are essential features of festivals organized by the government for the benefit of tourists.**

CALENDARS AND FESTIVALS

The calendar used in most of the world is the Gregorian calendar. It divides the year into a number of fixed days and months with an extra day being added every four years (leap year) to allow for the difference between the calendar year of 365 days and the actual time it takes for the Earth to circle the Sun (which is just a little longer). Most Christian festivals, with the important exception of Easter, are based on the Gregorian solar calendar. Christmas is always on December 25 and New Year's Day on January 1.

Most Muslim festivals are based on the moon's rotation around the Earth, following what is called a lunar calendar. There are still 12 months, of either 29 or 30 days, but the lunar year is 10 or 11 days shorter than the Gregorian solar year. As a result, Muslim festivals are not held at the same time each year; the dates vary, moving through the calendar and completing a cycle in about 33 years.

THE ISLAMIC CALENDAR

Month	No. of days	Month	No. of days
Muharram	30	Rajab	30
Safar	29	Shaban	30
Rabi 1	30	Ramadan	30
Rabi 2	29	Shawwal	29
Jumada 1	30	Dhu al-Qadah	30
Juamda 2	29	Dhu al-Hijjah	29 or 30

ISLAMIC FESTIVALS

1 Muharram	New Year's Day, starting on the day celebrating Mohammed's departure from Mecca to Medina in 622
10 Muharram	Ashura, the anniversary of the martyr Hussein's death
12 Rabi	Birthday of Mohammed in 572
27 Rajab	Night of Ascent of Mohammed to Heaven
1 Ramadan	Beginning of the month of fasting between sunrise and sunset
27 Ramadan	Night of Power, celebrating the sending down of the Koran to Mohammed
1 Shawwal	Feast of Breaking the Fast (Eid al-Fitr), celebrating the end of Ramadan
10 Dhu al-Hijjah	Feast of the Sacrifice (Eid al-Adha)

Crowds watch Shiite Muslims in a procession, many of them in clothes stained with their own blood.

RAMADAN

Muslims look forward to Ramadan ("rah-mah-DAHN"), the ninth month of the Islamic calendar, which is a month of fasting. They do not see it as something onerous to be endured. Fasting during the day provides a reason for feasting at night, and in Lebanon Ramadan is characterized by lively and joyful nights. The spirit of sharing is evident, and it is not uncommon for people to stay up all night and sleep during the afternoon.

EID AL-FITR

Eid al-Fitr, which marks the end of the fasting month, begins on the first day of the 10th month and lasts four days. It is celebrated by large family meals, which all members of an extended family make every effort to attend. Towards the end of Ramadan, the family home is thoroughly cleaned in preparation. If there is money for new clothes or new furniture this is the time the shopping will be done.

EID AL-ADHA

Eid al-Adha is called the Feast of the Sacrifice because it commemorates Abraham's willingness to sacrifice his son. Muslims slaughter a sheep on the feast day and give a portion of the meat to the poor. Celebrations tend to be quieter than at Eid al-Fitr.

ASHURA

The Shiites mourn the murder of Hussein, Prophet Mohammed's grandson, in the first 10 days of Muharram. On the last day, they reenact the murder and walk in a procession, which draws crowds to scenes of self-flagellation, sometimes with sharp objects that draw blood.

Eid al-Fitr is the most festive period of the year for Lebanese Muslims as it signifies the glorious culmination of a period of spiritual cleansing and purification. The festival period is a very social occasion and visits are made to the homes of in-laws and close friends.

Santa Claus, sometimes called Papa Noel in Lebanon, makes his appearance in shopping complexes like this one in Beirut.

CHRISTIAN FESTIVALS

The major Christian festivals of Christmas and Easter are celebrated in Lebanon in the same manner as in the West.

At Christmas time, trees are decorated and presents purchased for family and friends. On December 25 churches are packed with worshipers and midnight Mass is celebrated in most of them. It is a time for family reunions.

January 6 marks the Epiphany, a religious festival that commemorates the showing of the infant Jesus to the Magi, the manifestation of the divinity of Christ at his baptism, and his first miracle at Cana. It is still a tradition in places to prepare special Epiphany cakes to mark the occasion. They are also known as finger biscuits because of their shape. They are made in a special syrup consisting of sugar, lemon juice, rose water, and orange blossom water, mixed together and simmered until quite concentrated. The biscuits are soaked in this syrup and then fried in vegetable oil.

Easter is marked by processions. On Palm Sunday, the Sunday before Easter, families parade with their children carrying branches of palm leaves, flowers, and candles. Easter Sunday begins at midnight with another procession of families, led by a priest, to the front door of the unlighted church. He knocks loudly, calling out for the door to be opened so that the "King of Glory" can enter. He is refused. He knocks and makes his demand three times before the door is opened and the lights come on.

INDEPENDENCE DAY

Independence Day, November 22, is marked by national celebrations. For a country that has been at war with itself for so long, a day of national celebration is especially important. The day had little meaning during the 1980s, but now it has great significance.

Beirut is the center of Independence Day celebrations. The day is a national holiday and there are parades through the city center. People use the public holiday to visit their families and friends and celebratory meals are enjoyed.

THE BAALBEK FESTIVAL

Before the civil war erupted in 1975, Baalbek was the location for a major arts festival, held between mid-June and early September each year. It was the most prestigious festival in the country and always attracted tourists and visitors from all over the world. The success of the festival was partly due to its unique setting, an evocative background of ancient classical ruins, and partly due to world-class performances of local and international artistes. Plans are under way to relaunch the festival; it is probably only a matter of time before the Baalbek Festival resumes its place in the Lebanese calendar of the arts.

Lebanese folk dances, especially the *dabke*, with its themes based on stories of village life, were always featured in the festival. International symphony orchestras and ballet troupes were another regular feature at the festival. An evening ballet performance, with the dancers silhouetted against the temple ruins, was usually one of the festival highlights.

Music festivals were once a regular part of Lebanese culture, and the historical sites were popular venues. The Beit-ed-Din music festival is one of the few that has started again. One of the most prestigious music festivals was the one held at Baalbek and there are plans to revive this.

FOOD

LEBANESE FOOD SHARES CERTAIN SIMILARITIES with the cuisines of other Middle East countries. Common ingredients include lamb, eggplant, chickpeas, yogurt, garlic, mint, and olive oil combinations. In Lebanon, however, they are combined and prepared in a way that helps to make Lebanese food especially delicious.

FAVORITES

Three dishes form the staples of many meals: *felafel*, *hummus*, and *fuul*.

Felafel ("FEHL-a-fehl") are deep-fried balls of chickpea paste mixed with spices and pickled vegetables or tomatoes. It is usually eaten as a sandwich with Arabic bread. The meat equivalent of a *felafel* is *shawarma* ("shah-WAHR-mah"). Food stalls serving these are often found on city sidewalks. The meat for *shawarma* is sliced off a vertical spit and then squeezed into the bread and covered to overflowing with pickled vegetables or tomatoes.

Hummus ("HUM-us"), like *felafel*, uses chickpeas ground into a paste but mixed with lemon, sesame oil, and garlic. It is not as spicy as *felafel*. *Fuul* ("FU-ul"), a paste made from fava beans, garlic, and lemon, is often eaten with the oil used to cook it.

A very popular dish, which could lay claim to being the national dish, is *kibbih* ("KIBB-ee"), sometimes also spelled *kibbe*. It is made from deep-fried balls of meat and cracked wheat, which are often stuffed with more meat before being fried with onions.

Above: **Felafels**, savory bread, and cabbage rolls are served with a *hummus* dip.

Opposite: **A shop owner displays varieties of** *baklava*, **a pastry that is drenched in syrup and filled with honey and nuts.**

MEALS

Lebanese lunches and dinners tend to be leisurely affairs. A formal meal begins with an appetizer, often a salad, accompanied by *tabbouleh* ("tah-BOOL-uh"), a delicious mixture of chopped onions, parsley, cracked wheat, and tomatoes. A variety of dips will appear on the table, including *hummus*, *lebni* (a thick yogurt dip), and *baba ghanuj*, which is made of eggplant.

The main dish is usually lamb, which may be cooked in a variety of ways: stewed with okra, grilled as spicy chops, cubed on skewers—but nearly always served with rice. It may be served as *kefta*, a spicy ground meat mixed with chopped parsley and onions. After lamb, chicken is the most popular meat.

The traditional accompaniment to most Lebanese meals is a bread called *khobez* ("KOH-bez"), usually oval-shaped and always served hot, which is found in many Arab countries. Outside of the Middle East this bread is called pita bread. It is used both as a spoon for scooping up food and as a sponge for soaking up sauce or gravy on the plate. An informal meal at lunchtime often consists of mashed lamb or chicken sandwiched inside a piece of *khobez* and flavored with onions and spices.

As a general rule, Lebanese meals are not highly structured. There is often no clear distinction between appetizers and main meals. There is certainly no food code that sets out in what order particular dishes can be eaten. People like to mix and match their dishes in an informal manner.

MEZZE *Mezze* ("MEZ") is a varied spread of hot and cold hors d'oeuvres that can include a large number of dishes; so many, that when they are laid out on individual plates they form a complete and very substantial meal. Some of the more popular dishes include mashed beans, spicy meat balls, small parcels of rice and meat wrapped in grape leaves, hot and cold salads, seafood, *hummus*, and pistachios. Another common dish found in a *mezze* is shish-kebab, or skewered cubes of spiced lamb, peppers, and onions.

A particularly savory *mezze* dish consists of crushed almonds, cashews, and walnuts mixed with garlic, onions, cayenne pepper, and spices. It is called *job mahrouse* ("JOHR MAH-roose").

BAKED KIBBIH

This recipe for baked *kibbih* makes about 30 pieces.

1 pound ($^1/_2$ kg) ground lamb or beef	$^1/_4$ teaspoon black pepper
half a cup of bulgar (crushed wheat)	$^1/_4$ teaspoon ground cinnamon
1 onion, chopped	2 tablespoons dried parsley
2 tablespoons water	2 tablespoons walnuts or pine nuts
$^1/_4$ teaspoon ground allspice	1 tablespoon peanut oil

Mix the meat, bulgar, onion, water, allspice, pepper, cinnamon, and parsley in a food processor. Blend until the mixture forms a soft dough.

Preheat oven to 350°F (175°C).

Place half of the mixture in a 9-inch (23 cm) baking dish and sprinkle the nuts on top. Place the other half of the mixture over the nuts.

Cut into half-inch portions. Brush the surface with peanut oil. Bake for half an hour until firm and brown.

Right: **A man slices off pieces of grilled lamb, which he will serve with a salad and bread.**

Opposite: **A quick and inexpensive snack of chickpeas flavored with lemon and seasoned with spices is available at most street corners in Beirut.**

EATING OUT

A common sight outside restaurants is a spit for roasting chicken before cooking it in large ovens. Barbecued chicken is a favorite of the Lebanese. Lamb is often grilled over charcoal, as with *kebabs* ("KUH-bahbs"), which are eaten all over the Middle East. The spicy minced lamb is pressed onto skewers before being grilled and served with bread and a side dish, which is often a salad.

In the city, on the sidewalks or by the roadside, stand makeshift tables on wheels. Each holds some instant food that Lebanese stop to buy and savor on the spot to kill hunger pangs between meals. Breads, *felafel,* or simply chickpeas flavored with lemon and spices, together with some squares of paper to hold these ingredients, are all the entrepreneur needs to start business.

KITCHENS

The rural Lebanese cooks at a wood-fed stove. She prepares her dough and bakes it at home on a convex metal dome over a wood-fed fire or takes it to the village bakery, where it is baked for a fee. Urban kitchens are like Western ones, with appliances for preparing and cooking food.

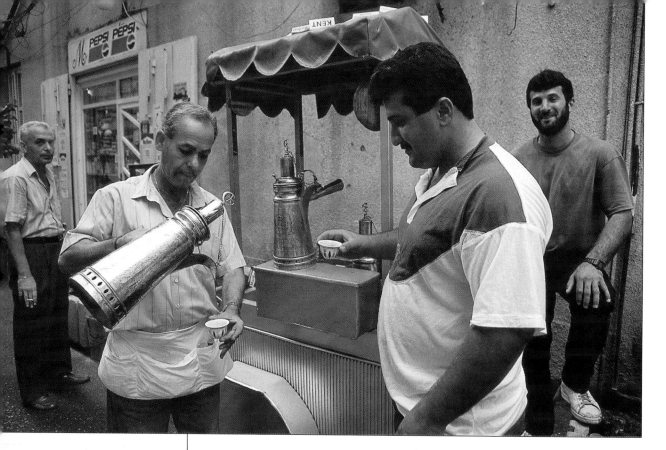

Lebanese have a choice
of soda and Arabic coffee
at this street stall.

DRINKS

Tea and coffee are the most popular drinks, but both are a lot stronger than their equivalents in the West. Another difference is that both drinks are served in tiny cups. Tea is often served in small glasses, sometimes flavored with mint. A generous amount of sugar is nearly always mixed with the tea. Coffee is also sweetened before serving. Strong Turkish coffee is preferred, and this has a remarkably thick and almost muddy appearance. The last mouthful in a cup is often not drunk, especially by non-Lebanese, not surprising since the dregs have been compared to silt by those unaccustomed to its thickness!

Lebanese enjoy drinking an Arabic coffee, often flavored with cardamom. It is served in tiny cups without handles that hold little more than a mouthful. Refills, poured from a silver or brass pot, continue until the drinker signals "enough" by placing a hand over the top of the cup.

The most common alcoholic drink is *arak*; when diluted with water, it turns a milky white color. Wine is also made in Lebanon and drunk with meals. In rural areas water is the most common thirst quencher. Dotted

SWEET DESSERTS

Like the coffee, desserts rarely come any sweeter than the Lebanese variety. A favorite Lebanese dessert is *baklava* ("BAHK-lah-vah"), a light flaky pastry filled with honey and chopped nuts and drenched in rose-flavored syrup. There are a number of variations to *baklava*, all characterized by the same syrupy richness. Less sweet is a milk custard made with pine nuts and almonds. Semolina cakes, sometimes filled with walnuts or dates, are often cooked at home as a dessert.

around the countryside, at gas stations and in village centers, are earthenware jugs known as *bre* ("BREE"). These are filled with fresh water and available to anyone who needs a drink.

Other nonalcoholic drinks include fresh fruit and vegetable juices. *Limonada* ("LIM-on-AH-DAH") is a fresh lemon squash that is popular, as is *jellab* ("JELL-ahb"), which is made from raisins and served with pine nuts. Various yogurts are also drunk.

All manner of sweets are available at this patisserie in Sidon (Sayda).

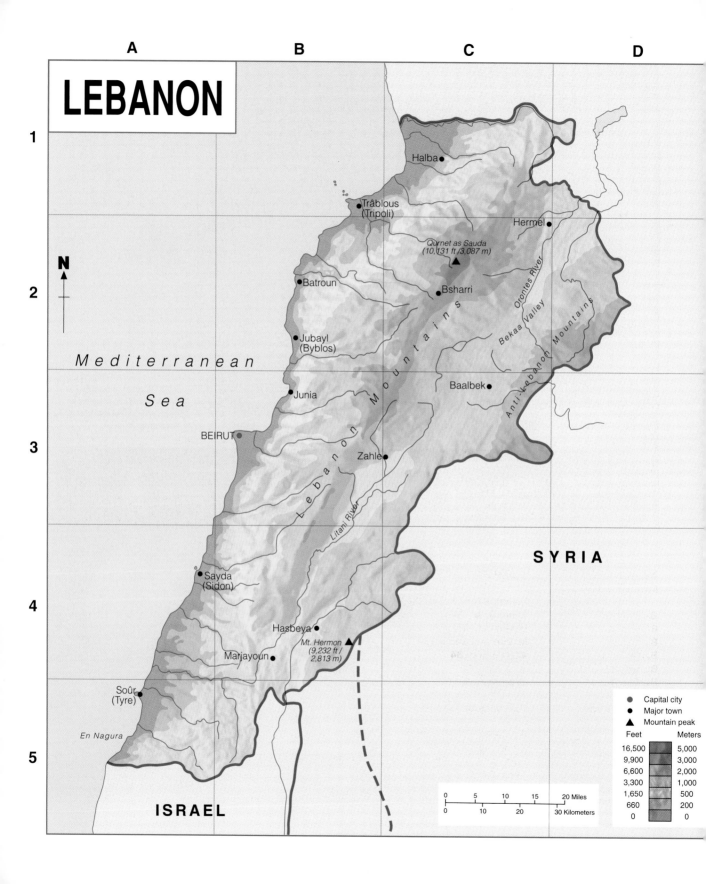

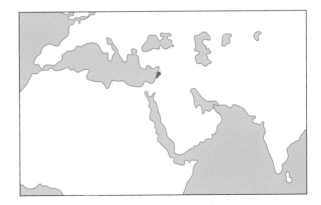

QUICK NOTES

OFFICIAL NAME
Republic of Lebanon

LAND AREA
3,950 sq. miles (10,230 sq. kilometers)

HIGHEST POINT
Qurnet as Sauda (10,131 ft / 3,087 m)

POPULATION
3.7 million (estimated)

CAPITAL
Beirut

MAJOR TOWNS
Beirut, Sidon, Tripoli, Tyre, Zahle

NATIONAL FLAG
Green and brown cedar tree in the center of a white stripe, with a red stripe on either side.

NATIONAL ANTHEM
Kulluna lil Watan (All of Us for the Homeland)

GOVERNMENT
A National Assembly of 128 members, elected by universal suffrage. A president, elected by the National Assembly every six years, must be a Maronite Christian. The prime minister must be a Sunni Muslim.

CURRENCY
Lebanese pound, divided into 100 piasters
1,592 pounds = US$1

MAIN EXPORTS
Agricultural products, chemicals, textiles, precious and semiprecious metals and jewelry.

CLIMATE
Mild winters, with snow on high ground, and hot summers with high humidity on the coast.

OFFICIAL LANGUAGES
Arabic, French

MAJOR RELIGIONS
Islam and Christianity

MAJOR FESTIVALS
Muslim: First of Muharram, Ashura, Eid al-Fitr, Eid al-Adha
Christian: Easter, Christmas

IMPORTANT ANNIVERSARIES
Independence Day, November 22
Arab League Anniversary, March 22

ETHNIC DIVISIONS
Arab 94%, Armenian 5%, Others 1%

POPULATION DENSITY
884 people per square mile;
84% in urban areas, 16% in rural areas

POLITICAL LEADERS
Rafiq Hariri, prime minister since the end of the civil war in 1990
Elias Hrawi, president since 1989

GLOSSARY

Abbasid ("ah-BAH-sid")
Dynasty of Arab rulers that ruled Lebanon from A.D. 750 to 1250.

arak ("ah-RUCK")
The national drink, a liquor distilled from grapes and flavored with anise.

confession
A Lebanese community defined by religion.

Druze ("DROOS")
A Middle East Muslim sect living mostly in the mountainous regions of Lebanon and neighboring Syria. The name is also spelt "Druse."

felafel ("FEHL-a-fehl")
Spicy, deepfried balls of chickpea paste mixed with spices and vegetables.

Hizbollah
Radical Muslim organization that continues to oppose Israel.

hummus ("HUM-us")
Chickpea paste mixed with lemon, sesame oil, and garlic.

Levant
Countries bordering the eastern shores of the Mediterranean Sea.

Maronites
Members of the Uniate Catholics, originating in Syria in the seventh century, and now chiefly found in Lebanon.

mezze ("MEZ")
Wide-ranging spread of hot and cold appetizers.

militia
A military force, especially one that is formed from the civilian population as a result of an emergency situation.

muezzin ("moo-EZ-in")
Mosque official who calls worshipers to prayer.

Phoenician
A Semitic people of ancient Phoenicia, a land that included modern Lebanon.

Ramadan ("rah-ma-DAHN")
The ninth month of the Muslim year, observed by fasting between sunrise and sunset.

Shiites ("SHE-ites")
An Islamic sect, originating with the murder of Ali, Prophet Mohammed's son-in-law and nephew. The Shiites were supporters of Ali's claim to be the Islamic leader after Mohammed.

Sunni ("SOO-nee")
Mainstream Islamic sect throughout the Middle East, comprising 80% of all Muslims in the world. This group differs from Shiite Muslims in the matter of Prophet Mohammed's successor.

'ud ("OOD")
Musical instrument, forerunner of the lute.

Umayyad ("oo-MY-ahd")
A dynasty of Arab rulers, based in Damascus, that ruled Lebanon from A.D. 630 to 750.

BIBLIOGRAPHY

Cleary, Thomas (translator). *The Essential Koran*. San Francisco: Harper, 1994.

Foster, Leila Merrell. *Enchantment of the World: Lebanon*. Chicago: Children's Press, 1992.

Frenea, Elizabeth and Robert. *The Arab World: Personal Encounters*. Anchor, 1985.

Lebanon in Pictures. Visual Geography Series. Minneapolis: Lerner Publications, 1988

Maalouf, Amin. *The Crusaders Through History*. Schocken Books, 1987.

Marston, Elsa. *Lebanon: New Light in an Ancient Land*. New York: Dillon Press, 1994.

Musallam, Basim. *The Rabas: A Living History*. Collins/Harvill, 1983.

INDEX

INDEX

INDEX

names, 88
nargileh, 104

occupations, 65
oil, 15, 49
olives, 12–13, 16, 44
Ottomans, 14, 15, 24, 25, 51, 73, 87, 93, 98

Palestine Liberation Organization (PLO), 27, 28
Palestinians, 27, 28, 33, 36, 37, 53, 56–57, 58, 75, 81
parliament, 26, 31, 37
Phoenicians, 3, 11, 15, 16, 20–21, 51, 91, 92–93
pilgrimage, 76, 78–79
poetry, 100
pollution, 41, 66–67
population, 14, 31, 52–53, 62, 65, 75
proverbs, 51, 63, 105
publishing, 100

Ramadan, 78, 109, 110, 111
Ramses II, 20
refugees/refugee camps, 27, 33, 36, 37, 39, 56, 57, 62, 64, 65, 67, 81
rivers
    Litani, 8, 9, 44
    Orontes, 9, 10
Romans, 14, 17, 19, 21–22, 23, 83, 93
Russia, 25

saints' days, 113
Salman, Nour, 100
sculpture, 20
shawarma, 115
Sherfe monastery, 87
Shihabs, 24, 92
Shiites, 26, 31, 32, 33, 35, 57, 75, 80, 81, 99, 101, 110, 111
see also Hizbollah
skiing, 7, 106–107
Solomon, 11, 16
South Lebanese Army (SLA), 31, 32, 34

South Lebanon, 34, 35, 61, 62, 97
sponge fishing, 15
sports, 57, 106–107
Sunnis, 31, 68, 75, 80, 81
sweets, 121
Syria/Syrians, 3, 7, 8, 9, 10, 20, 21, 23, 26, 28, 29, 32, 33, 35, 37, 49, 53, 55, 58, 75, 82, 96

tabbouleh, 116
Taif Agreement, 29, 33, 58
tea, 120
tourism, 7, 39, 47, 97, 104, 109, 113
trade, 39, 45, 49
Turkey, 10, 52, 82, 83, 98

Umayyads, 23
United Nations, 27, 56, 58, 64
United States, 26, 45, 47, 58, 59, 72, 73, 96, 104

values, 72
vegetables, 8, 44, 121

wars
    civil war, 3, 14, 25, 26, 28–29, 31, 32, 36, 37, 39, 41, 42, 43, 46, 47, 48, 51, 52, 56, 58, 59, 62, 63, 66, 72, 88, 91, 99, 100, 101, 113
    World War I, 25, 51, 82, 85
welfare, 35
women, 54, 65, 68–69, 71, 72, 77, 99, 104
writers, 91, 100–101

zajal, 100

PICTURE CREDITS

Andes Press Agency: 3, 78
Björn Klingwall: 18, 19, 62, 63, 112, 118
Camera Press: 17, 22, 28, 29, 30, 32, 33, 38, 48, 53, 57, 59, 61, 65, 74, 77, 92, 102
Christine Osborne: 5, 12, 34, 43, 46, 47, 51, 64, 66, 67, 68, 70, 72, 80, 90, 98, 114, 115, 116, 119
HBL Network: 1, 58, 95, 96, 97, 107, 108
Hulton-Deutsch: 20, 23, 25, 26, 27
Hutchison: 8, 24, 86, 89, 99, 105
Life File: 31, 40
Reuters: 35, 36, 37, 56, 69, 106, 110
R. Holzbachová & P. Bénet: 4, 6, 7, 10, 11, 13, 14, 16, 39, 41, 44, 45, 49, 50, 52, 54, 55, 60, 71, 73, 75, 79, 81, 82, 83, 84, 85, 91, 93, 94, 101, 103, 104, 117, 120, 121, 123